NEW WORLD MONEY

Teeka Tiwari

Editor, Palm Beach Research Group

What Some of Our Readers Are Saying About Teeka Tiwari's "New World Money"

- *"I'm up almost $1 million on your recommendations. I've never traded on any market before. So many thanks to Teeka."*—**Jim R.**

- *"All I can say is thank you, thank you, thank you! I've never seen gains like this in my life. My only regret is I didn't act on your recommendations sooner."*—**Riz M.**

- *"We are up 474% annualized! It's only been 18 days! Thank you, Teeka and team!"*—John and Sandy M.

- *"I just want to personally extend my thanks to Teeka and the team. I'm up 396% and about to pull every dollar of my original investment out and let the 'house money' grow!"*—**John B.**

- *"I placed about $300 in. Was left nearly speechless last night when I discovered that my $300 had grown to over $43,300. I have never heard of such gains in such a short time frame."*—**Jon M.**

- *"I was just admiring your portfolio. It is like nothing I have ever seen before—I mean nothing bearing any semblance to ANY portfolio page results I have EVER seen before. Not sure how to thank you... but THANK YOU!"*—**William T.**

- *"My $20,000 initial stake is now over $100,000. Needless to say, I'm pretty happy with your research."* —**George W.**

- *"Your information has been absolutely outstanding. I started investing in your recommendations back in December 2016, and as you know, returns have been mind-blowing. I never imagined the results would have occurred so quickly. I can't thank you enough."* —**Raymond W.**

- *"Just a note of thanks. I am now close to $200,000 after my initial funding of $8,000. Couldn't be happier. Keep them coming."*—**Pete A.**

- *"I pulled a bunch out of the stock market and bought [one of Teeka's recommendations] at $88. Was up over 21 times on my trade. This stuff is changing my life."* —**James R.**

- *"Teeka, you have made me so much money. I initially invested between $6,000–8,000. My investments are now worth over $43,000. They have changed my life and the life of my family. Thank you for all your hard work."*—**Jose H.**

- *"I wanted to send a big thank you. Turned $600 into $10,000 in less than a year. Guess I'm a fan for life now."*—**Ron L.**

NEW WORLD
MONEY

Teeka Tiwari

Editor, Palm Beach Research Group

PALM BEACH RESEARCH GROUP

ISBN 978-1-5323-5236-2

Published by:
The Palm Beach Research Group
Delray Beach, Florida

www.palmbeachgroup.com

PALM BEACH RESEARCH GROUP

About the Palm Beach Research Group

The Palm Beach Research Group is an independent financial publishing company based in Delray Beach, Florida. It publishes various advisories that provide stock, options, and income recommendations—as well as non-market wealth-building advice—to more than 230,000 readers.

When founders Mark Ford and Tom Dyson launched the Palm Beach Research Group in 2011, they wanted to create a publishing company unlike any other.

Most financial advisories are little more than stock "tip sheets." Mark and Tom had a different vision for their company. They wanted to provide subscribers a comprehensive wealth-building plan; one that would guide readers along the path to real, sustained financial prosperity.

In 2014, Mark and Tom brought in retired hedge fund manager Teeka Tiwari to the team.

Together, the trio focused the Palm Beach Research Group on three key areas: safe income, safe growth, smart speculation, and comprehensive 360-degree wealth building.

Specifically, they've combined Teeka and Tom's experience in the financial markets with Mark's success as a serial entrepreneur and real estate investor to achieve their goal—a holistic, wealth-building publishing company.

Services now include:

- Stock market investments (long term and trading)
- Cash-generating options strategies
- Rental real estate investing strategies
- "Outside the market" ideas for generating additional active income
- Credit repair strategies
- Entrepreneurial guidelines on starting your own business
- Retirement lifestyle guidelines
- "Smart speculations" in alternative investments

And much more...

Each service supports the central mission of the Palm Beach Research Group:

Help readers get richer every single year.

To learn more about the Palm Beach Research Group, visit www.palmbeachgroup.com/about.

About the Author

 **Teeka Tiwari** is the editor of *The Palm Beach Letter*. He epitomizes the American dream. Growing up in the foster care system in the United Kingdom, Teeka came to the United States at age 16 with just $150 in his pocket and the clothes on his back. By 18, he had become the youngest employee at Lehman Brothers. Two years later, he shattered convention by becoming the youngest vice president in the history of Shearson Lehman.

In 1998, he made a small fortune going short during the Asian crisis. But then, he "got greedy" (in his own words) and hung on for too long.

Within a three-week span, he lost all he had made—and everything else he owned. He was ultimately compelled to file personal bankruptcy.

Two years after losing everything, Teeka rebuilt his wealth from the markets and went on to launch a successful hedge fund. After these events, he developed a newfound appreciation for risk. He made risk management his No. 1 priority. Now a retired hedge fund manager, Teeka's personal mission is to help teach individual investors how to grow their money safely.

Teeka has been a regular contributor to the FOX Business Network and has appeared on FOX News Channel, CNBC, ABC's *Nightline*, *The Daily Show with Jon Stewart*, and international television networks.

Table of Contents

Chapter 1:
Bitcoin Rises From the Ashes

You are looking at a live picture of Lehman Brothers' 158-year-old firm—born pre-industrial revolution and surviving the Great Depression...

Lehman Brothers will file for bankruptcy this evening under circumstances that, without the government's assistance, sources tell us would almost certainly result in significant market disruption.

– CNBC special report, September 14, 2008

I trust you remember what happened next.

The credit market's liquidity evaporated. The S&P was cut in half. 30 million jobs were shed. U.S. households lost $16 trillion worth of financial wealth. More than one million homes were lost in foreclosure.

Fear and panic spread. Some said the stock market was going to zero. Some said this was the end of capitalism. Others said it was the end of human civilization.

The U.S. government rushed in with a $700 billion bail-out package for banks it deemed "too big to fail." With the stroke of a pen, taxpayers were on the hook for Wall Street's reckless behavior.

But it didn't stop at $700 billion.

The Federal Reserve (the Fed) went on to inject $3.7 trillion into the financial system over the next several years.

The Fed used this new money to do two things.

First, it purchased U.S. Treasury bonds in bulk to artificially suppress interest rates.

Second, it purchased the toxic mortgage debt from Wall Street, thus transferring bad debt from the banking sector to the public sector... to the taxpayer.

This was sold as heroic. Fed Chairman Ben Bernanke called it "The Courage to Act" in his memoir.

But a few people out there weren't so sure. They had to ask: Where did that $3.7 trillion come from?

And the answer they found was rather simple. It came from nowhere. Well, to be more specific, it came from a journal entry on the books of the Federal Reserve.

The Fed is very honest about how this works. They tell you right on their website. The Fed basically writes a check "against itself" to create money for whatever purpose it deems necessary.

Now most people don't question this. It's not even on their radar. But those who understand basic economics realize something very important: Value is driven by supply and demand. As supply goes up, value tends to go down.

In other words, an item needs to be relatively scarce and relatively useful for it to have value. This is true of anything... especially money.

The median household income in the United States is about $53,000 per year according to the U.S. Census Bureau. You need at least six decimal points before your Excel spreadsheet can compare this $53,000 figure to the $3.7 trillion that the Fed created from nothing.

What does that say about your monetary system?

This caused a few people to protest the Wall Street banks. And a few others protested the government.

They learned pretty quickly that their protests were doomed from the beginning. Brute force and opposition is not what changes institutional systems.

Systems theorist Buckminster Fuller observed this dynamic early in the 20th century. Here's Bucky:

> *You never change things by fighting the existing reality. To change something, build a new model that makes the existing model obsolete.*

But this was not a new discovery.

Famed artist Michelangelo understood this way back in Europe's High Renaissance period. "Criticize by creating" is how Michelangelo put it.

Let's turn our attention back to 2008.

Lehman Brothers has collapsed. Wall Street is in shambles. Fear and panic is spreading across the country... and across the globe.

In this environment, a curious message appeared on an obscure mailing list dedicated to the study of cryptography. The date was November 1, 2008. The author was Satoshi Nakamoto.

> *I've been working on a new electronic cash system that's fully peer-to-peer, with no trusted third party... The main properties:*

Double-spending is prevented with a peer-to-peer network.

No mint or other trusted parties.

Participants can be anonymous.

New coins are made from Hashcash style proof-of-work.

The proof-of-work for new coin generation also powers the network to prevent double-spending...

I had to write all the code before I could convince myself that I could solve every problem, then I wrote the paper... You're already right about most of your assumptions... Governments are good at cutting off the heads of centrally controlled networks like Napster, but pure P2P networks like Gnutella and Tor seem to be holding their own...

Bitcoin was born. It rose from the ashes of the worst financial crisis since the Great Depression.

But to truly understand bitcoin, the world's first digital currency (or cryptocurrency), you must also understand money. What is it? Where does it come from? Where has it been?

Think about it. What is money?

We know what money does—it buys things. But can we define it?

Is it a green piece of paper with numbers, words, and symbols printed on it? Is it a card with your name, a string of numbers, and a bank logo on it?

Or is that just a piece of paper and a piece of plastic?

The short answer is that money is a unit of account that serves as a medium of exchange. But this is an incomplete view. To be sustainable, money must have several definitive characteristics.

- **Money must be durable.** It must serve as a store of value over long periods of time.

- **Money must be portable.** It must be easy to move money around—either in person or electronically.

- **Money must be divisible.** You must be able to break money down into consistent smaller units that add up to consistent larger units. In other words, you must be able to make "change" out of your money.

- **Money must be fungible.** It must be interchangeable. Each monetary unit must be consistently the same.

Any item that has these properties can serve as money.

Now that we know what money is, we need to figure out where it comes from... and where it has been.

As it turns out, this story is far more interesting than you would think.

A Brief Monetary History

Prior to the 20th century, most of the world operated on the gold standard through which international trades were settled in gold.

While not perfect, the classical gold standard kept nations mostly honest in their financial dealings with each other. It also forced nations to live within their means.

Large trade deficits had to be settled in gold, which drained gold from the nation's reserves. Conversely, a trade surplus added gold to the nation's reserves. This system placed limits on national debt.

World War I effectively put an end to the classical gold standard in 1914. To finance the war effort, the countries involved "printed" new money that was not convertible to gold. Trade settlement in gold was suspended indefinitely.

Most nations attempted to go back to the gold standard once the war was over. But the excessive money-printing caused their national currencies to diminish in value significantly. That meant nations would have to peg their currency to gold at a higher ratio than before, thus admitting the currency had lost value. Instead, the war combatants scrapped the gold standard.

During the same period, the shift towards central planning in America led to the creation of the Federal Reserve System in 1913.

The Federal Reserve is not a government agency. It is actually a group of private central banks that act as one unit. The U.S. government granted the Fed a legal monopoly on the issuance of currency.

In other words, the Fed is permitted to create U.S. dollars as it sees fit. Anyone else who attempts this will go to jail for counterfeiting.

The Federal Reserve was also tasked with being a "banker's bank," which meant the Fed would loan newly created money to commercial banks that got in trouble. They thought this would make the system stronger.

Instead, it created "moral hazard" within the banking system. Commercial banks knew that the Fed would bail them out if needed... so lending standards diminished over time. It became easier and easier for risky borrowers to get a loan.

This is the dynamic that ultimately caused the financial crisis of 2008. Wall Street, backed by the Fed—and the government—made too many loans to too many risky borrowers. Then it chopped up those risky loans and packaged them into complex derivatives.

And they kept doing this until it all blew up in 2008.

Rather than learn their lesson, the monetary authorities transferred the banking losses to the public with bailouts and quantitative easing programs to keep the system going.

But we need to back up for a minute. Those bank bailouts and quantitative easing programs would not have been possible 100 years ago. There were several changes to the monetary system that had to occur first.

The U.S. dollar was backed by gold when the Fed was first created in 1913. Americans could trade their dollars for gold anytime they wanted to at first.

But then, in 1933, President Franklin Delano Roosevelt (FDR) issued an executive order that made it illegal for Americans to own gold. In fact, Americans were required to sell their gold to the government for $20.67.

After it had bought all the gold domestically, the U.S. Treasury announced that foreign central banks would still be able to trade dollars for gold... but it raised the conversion rate to $35 per ounce.

This influx of gold for cheap gave the U.S. government a strong seat at the Bretton Woods conference in 1944. At this conference, representatives from 44 nations met in Bretton Woods, New Hampshire to discuss a new international monetary system.

They agreed upon the "Bretton Woods System" that established the U.S. dollar as the world's reserve currency.

As the world's sole reserve currency, the dollar replaced gold as the medium for international trade settlement. This meant that all international goods would be bought and sold in U.S. dollars... no matter which nations were doing the buying and selling. The dollar would remain pegged to gold at $35 per ounce, and other nations could redeem their dollars for gold through the "gold window."

7

The dollar's convertibility into gold on demand was to serve as a "check" on the United States. The link to gold is what gave the other countries confidence in the U.S. dollar.

The Bretton Woods System bestowed an enormous privilege upon the United States because it created a global demand for dollars. All nations needed to hold U.S. dollars to facilitate foreign trade.

This dynamic made trade deficits irrelevant for the United States. Under the gold standard, trade deficits required the U.S. to send its gold to another country. Under Bretton Woods, trade deficits required the U.S. to send its dollars to another country. And the U.S. could just print new dollars to ship out if it needed to.

This artificial global demand for dollars is what powered Lyndon Johnson's "guns and butter" campaign that ramped up in the 1950s.

The U.S. military went to war with Korea and Vietnam overseas. That was the "guns" part. At the same time, the Great Society welfare programs launched domestically. That was the "butter."

These initiatives were extremely expensive. As they progressed, the U.S. government created more and more new dollars to pay for them.

But foreign countries took notice. They began to worry about the value of the dollars they were holding. And rumors of the U.S. unilaterally changing the gold conversion ratio spread.

Here's former French President Charles de Gaulle in 1965:

> *The fact that many countries accept as principle, dollars being as good as gold, for the payment of the differences existing to their advantage in the American balance of trade... this fact leads Americans to get into debt and to get into debt for free at the expense of other countries... We consider necessary that international trade be established*

as it was the case before the great misfortunes of the world, on an indisputable monetary base, and one that does not bear the mark of any particular country. Which base? In truth, no one sees how one could really have any standard criterion other than gold!

France and other concerned nations began to rapidly exchange their dollars for gold through the gold window. It was a global "bank run" on the dollar and gold rapidly flowed out of U.S. vaults.

By 1971, the U.S. Treasury only had enough gold to cover 22% of all dollars outstanding. It was about to run out of money.

The Birth of the Petrodollar

On August 15, 1971, President Richard Nixon closed the international gold window to stop the outflow of gold. Nixon assured the world that this closure would only be temporary.

"Your dollar will be worth just as much tomorrow as it is today," Nixon proclaimed on television with a straight face. "The effect of this action, in other words, will be to stabilize the dollar."

But Nixon had a trick up his sleeves.

Along with his Secretary of State Henry Kissinger, Nixon struck a deal with the Saudi Royal Family. The Saudis agreed to price all international oil sales exclusively in U.S. dollars. They would refuse settlement in all other currencies. In return, the U.S. would provide military protection and military-grade weapons.

This deal effectively kept the U.S. dollar as the world's reserve currency, even with the breakdown of the Bretton Woods System.

By 1975, all OPEC nations followed suit and agreed to settle oil trades exclusively in dollars. These were the largest oil producers in the world, and they only accepted dollars. Which meant all other countries still needed to obtain dollars to purchase oil.

This is where we stand today.

We are in the midst of a global experiment with fiat money.

Since 1971, the U.S. dollar and all other currencies have been *created from nothing by government decree.* That is the definition of "fiat" currency.

All restraints on currency creation have been removed.

It took a little while for governments to catch on. But throughout the 1980s, national governments realized they had unlimited money to spend.

And spend they did.

But their money-for-nothing policies were not without consequences. Prices for goods and services exploded across the board as new money flooded into the economy.

That is why the hamburger that cost $0.45 in 1971 costs $5 today.

The obscured fact is that this is not a case of rising prices. Your dollars are actually losing value over time—thus requiring more dollars to buy the same item. Price inflation is an artificial monetary event.

To come full circle, the U.S. dollar has lost 96% of its value since the Federal Reserve opened its doors in 1913. Stated another way, the dollar could purchase nearly 50 times more goods and services back in 1913 than it can today.

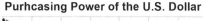

Purhcasing Power of the U.S. Dollar

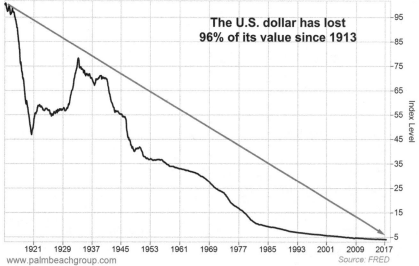

The U.S. dollar has lost
96% of its value since 1913

www.palmbeachgroup.com

Source: FRED

Despite Nixon's proclamation on national television, the value of the U.S. dollar fell off a cliff.

While incomes in general have also risen during the last 100 years, their rise has not kept pace with the dollar's loss of value. This is the primary reason households now require two wage earners to make financial ends meet.

The global experiment with fiat money has also led to an explosion of debt, especially in the Western economies and Japan. Without sound money restraint, nations have been able to finance deficits and run up enormous debt that can never possibly be paid back.

The United States' national debt has now eclipsed $19 trillion.

Here is the numerical representation of the U.S. debt:

$19,000,000,000,000

This is an incredible amount of money, especially given we are talking about the issuer of the world's reserve currency.

And it is not just the U.S. Every major country in the world has run up its sovereign debt bill significantly over the last thirty years.

On the Hook for $200 Trillion

But sovereign debt is only part of the story, and a sticky part at that.

Governments accumulate sovereign debt when they issue bonds... which, in the United States, is done through Treasury auctions.

The U.S. Treasury sells notes and bonds of various durations (2, 3, 5, 10 and 30 years) at "auction." The bonds are sold at a "market" rate of interest where the Treasury promises to make interest payments to the bondholder semi-annually for the length of the term, and then re-pay the principal balance upon maturity.

Here's the sticky part: National governments can easily "roll-over" their outstanding debt by issuing new bonds to pay off the old bonds when they come due. If market demand for the new issue falls short, the central bank can simply create more dollars to buy the new bonds.

That is the magic money machine. And it is how they kick the debt can further and further into the future.

Here's the other part of the story: unfunded sovereign liabilities far exceed sovereign debt around the world... especially in the U.S.

Unfunded sovereign liabilities are future expenses that governments have already committed to paying. The biggest of these are pension plans and health care programs—Social Security and Medicare in the U.S.

Generally Accepted Accounting Principles (GAAP) require private companies to report unfunded liabilities in their financial statements... but government gets a pass. So, you won't find these listed on any government balance sheet.

Boston University economist Laurence Kotlikoff estimates U.S. unfunded liabilities to be $222 trillion. The bulk of this comes from Social Security and Medicare.

It wasn't always this way. Social Security was solvent in its early years.

And it was a great deal for a lot of people who retired in the early stages of the program. Take the story of the first Social Security payee, Ida May, for example.

Ida paid a full $24.75 into the system before retiring. She lived to receive nearly $23,000 in retirement benefits. No one thought twice about this at the time because there were 42 workers for every person receiving Social Security benefits.

There are now 2.8 workers for every Social Security beneficiary. Simply put, there are no longer enough workers to pay for retirees. The difference is the unfunded liability.

Social Security is already running a $50 billion deficit annually. That is with most of the Baby Boomer generation still working.

This annual deficit will grow larger and larger as the Boomers retire. And demographics show that there will be 10,000 people in the United States turning 65 every single day for the next decade. That's a whole lot of people knocking on Social Security's door.

The Medicare system is not doing much better. Medicare is currently running a $30 billion deficit annually. Again, that deficit will grow larger as the Baby Boomers retire.

I am highlighting the U.S. government simply because of the dollar's supremacy in global finance. But they aren't the only culprits. Most developed nations have accrued unfunded liabilities to some degree.

The Magic Money Machine

Free market economists have been decrying this system since it came about with the Nixon shock in the 1970s. "It will never work," they said. "The feds will destroy the currency."

But the fiat money system is still chopping along nearly 50 years later. Fiat currencies have plummeted in value since this experiment began in 1971. But they haven't died.

The old free market economists could not foresee how the central bank would be used to crank out new money and lock away bad assets. They underestimated the power of the magic money machine.

Or perhaps they just confused inevitable with imminent.

The magic money machine cannot reverse course. The debt and unfunded liabilities accumulated can never be paid off. They can only be "rolled over" by creating more money and more debt. This guarantees that fiat currencies will continue to lose value every single year.

Which means the money you work so hard for will constantly lose value... forever. The magic money machine will never stop stealing purchasing power from you...

Up until 2009, there were no alternatives to this system. You were stuck holding paper money that was depreciating by the day. You were trapped in the rat-race.

No longer.

Bitcoin gives you a way out. With bitcoin, you can exit the abusive fiat money system. You can hold money that will grow in value over time because it is extremely scarce. And you can stop the magic money machine from stealing the value you work so hard to earn.

Bitcoin Since 2009

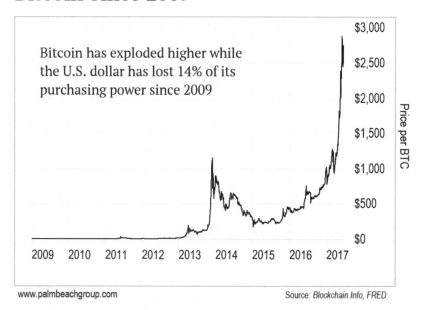

Bitcoin has exploded higher while the U.S. dollar has lost 14% of its purchasing power since 2009

www.palmbeachgroup.com

Source: Blockchain.Info, FRED

The abusive fiat money system creates a world in which you must work harder and harder just to maintain the same standard of living. It is impossible to save money because that money constantly loses value.

Bitcoin reverses this dynamic. It allows you to truly reap the fruits of your labor. And bitcoin makes it much easier to maintain, or even increase, your standard of living over time.

That is why I chuckle whenever I hear the objection: "But I can't buy my coffee with it."

One day you will be able to buy everything with bitcoin as easily as you swipe your credit card today. But that misses the entire point.

Bitcoin is not here to make shopping easier. It is not here to be a digital version of the dollar.

Bitcoin was born from the ashes of the 2008 financial crisis. It is here to give you a way out of the abusive fiat money system. It is here to hold the power institutions accountable for stealing your purchasing power. Bitcoin is here to empower you, as an individual.

Bitcoin gives you 100% control of your money. It makes you the President and CEO of your own bank—with all the power and responsibilities that entails.

In a moral system, hard work and dedication should pay off. You should be able to set concrete financial goals and then plan how you will achieve them.

That can't happen when your purchasing power is constantly stolen from you. It certainly can't happen when you are expected to bail-out failed banks and pay off debt you never incurred.

That's why Bitcoin is here—to level the playing field. Ultimately, bitcoin is going to give you back control of your financial destiny.

Chapter 2:
Bitcoin Will Change the Money System

Monetary policy is the process by which the size and growth rate of the money supply is governed. This is the single most important factor determining the health of an economy simply because money is half of every transaction.

Monetary policy has been managed by old men and women in stale suits sitting behind closed central bank doors for 100 years now. Despite their air of legitimacy, these central bankers have done nothing but rig the game in favor of the world's power institutions: governments and big banks.

We have already seen how the magic money machine is used to give governments unlimited spending power and to bail-out the big banks... all at the taxpayer's expense. There is another little nuance you should know about.

Every transaction between the U.S. government and the Federal Reserve has to flow through what's called a "primary dealer." Primary dealers are the only banks permitted to transfer money and securities between the government and the Fed. And they receive a commission on every transaction they facilitate.

Which means the big banks receive a cut of all new money created from thin air by the magic money machine. They directly profit from the U.S. government's debt binge.

This is why the fiat monetary system is inherently inflationary. Central banks around the world create money at will every single year. Then the value of that money goes down. Which means the cost of living goes up for everybody.

Some are worse than others, but every country's central bank does this to some degree.

Bitcoin is fundamentally different. Satoshi Nakamoto built a deflationary monetary system into the core of bitcoin's source code. New bitcoins are "mined" into existence per this monetary policy.

And bitcoin is a market-based system—there are no "insiders." Miners compete to solve the math problems necessary to mine for— i.e., create—bitcoins.

I'll give you a quick rundown of how it all works here... and if it starts sounding too complicated—don't worry. We'll discuss the blockchain in greater detail in Chapter 3.

The gist: Mining is the process of validating transactions and adding transaction records to bitcoin's public ledger, called the blockchain. These records are added to the blockchain in "blocks," hence the name.

The system is designed so that each new "block" is added to the larger "chain" roughly every 10 minutes. These records are public and they are permanent. There is no mechanism for altering the ledger in any way.

The blockchain is simultaneously maintained by thousands of mining rigs around the world. These mining rigs are each making trillions of calculations every single second... which makes bitcoin's mining network more powerful than 500 of the world's fastest supercomputers. And this also makes the bitcoin network practically impossible to hack.

Without getting too technical, it would take huge amounts of computing power and a lot of time to change a single transaction.

But Wasn't Bitcoin Hacked?

By now, you've probably seen a headline or two saying bitcoin was hacked.

There's an important distinction to be made here. The bitcoin blockchain has never been hacked. What has been hacked are exchanges such as Mt. Gox and Bitfinex. (You'll learn more about exchanges in later chapters.)

These centralized services are weak points in the bitcoin ecosystem. But don't worry; there are steps you can take to protect your funds.

First, never keep too much of your digital money on any cryptocurrency exchange. Second, consider using cold storage features to store your digital money offline.

Finally, you can store your bitcoins in a paper wallet. This takes your bitcoins offline and stores them on a physical document. Just make sure to store it in a very safe place.

Don't worry; we will go over everything you need to know about how to acquire, use, and store bitcoins safely in a later chapter.

Meanwhile, the decentralized network of miners would continuously confirm transactions and add new blocks on top of your targeted hack.

So even if you had the computing power to alter a transaction, you would not be able to do so before the network had already confirmed new blocks on top of your target. Thus, the network would disregard you entirely. Your change would not stick.

That is the beauty of the decentralized proof-of-work system. And that's why you can trust bitcoin to be a borderless, transnational, immutable, incorruptible, and censorship-resistant system. It has no other choice.

This image simplifies how the system works:

How Blockchain Works

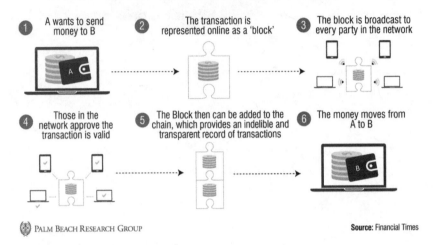

The bitcoin network relies on the mining process for security. That is mining's primary purpose.

The more computing power dedicated to mining, the more secure the bitcoin network becomes.

Naturally, there must be an incentive for people to use their computing power to secure the bitcoin network. The chance to "mine" new bitcoins into existence is that incentive.

Each block also contains all the fees associated with each transaction processed. The miners receive those fees in addition to the new bitcoins.

This puts everyone's financial interest in alignment.

Satoshi designed this system to harness the power of potentially billions of computers around the world for security purposes. That's far better than relying on a centralized entity with a single point of failure.

And that is where monetary policy comes back into the picture.

Bitcoin's total money supply is capped at 21 million. That is hardcoded and cannot change.

There will always be a new block mined roughly every 10 minutes. This is a constant that is managed by a self-adjusting "difficulty" level. Which means new bitcoins come into the network every 10 minutes or so.

The number of new bitcoins mined in each block decreases significantly over time, however. The new block reward size is "halved" every four years.

At first, each new block contained 50 bitcoins. The block reward was halved to 25 bitcoins in 2012. And it was halved to 12.5 bitcoins in 2016. Another "halving" will occur in 2020. Miners will only receive 6.25 new bitcoins per block at that point.

This process will continue through the year 2140 until all 21 million bitcoins have been mined into existence. In this way, bitcoin is much more akin to gold than fiat currency in terms of how new money enters the market.

Once all 21 million bitcoins have been mined, bitcoin miners will be paid fees from transactions on the network. This will be one incentive to keep them running the system.

To recap: Bitcoin is limited in supply, and it becomes exponentially more difficult to mine over time. These qualities produce the "scarcity" element necessary for any store of value.

Let's put this scarcity into perspective.

As I write, 16.4 million bitcoins have been mined since bitcoin was born. Remember, there are only 21 million bitcoins total... so 78% of all bitcoins that will ever exist are already here. Yet the last bitcoin will not be mined until the year 2140.

That is what a deflationary monetary system looks like. And that is why you can expect bitcoin's value to increase significantly over time.

Will It Catch On?

Here is what Satoshi had to say when bitcoin launched in 2009:

> *I would be surprised if 10 years from now, we're not using electronic currency in some way, now that we know a way to do it that won't inevitably get dumbed down when the trusted third party gets cold feet.*
>
> *It could get started in a narrow niche like reward points, donation tokens, currency for a game or micropayments for adult sites. Initially it can be used in proof-of-work applications for services that could almost be free but not quite...*
>
> *It might make sense just to get some in case it catches on. If enough people think the same way, that becomes a self-fulfilling prophecy. Once it gets bootstrapped, there are so many applications if you could effortlessly pay a few cents to a website as easily as dropping coins in a vending machine...*
>
> *I am sure that in twenty years there will either be very large Bitcoin transaction volume... or none.*

Eight years later, $1 billion worth of bitcoin transactions take place every single day.

Satoshi was wrong about the nature of the first mass-adopter transactions, however. He thought they would be for novelty, mostly irrelevant purchases.

He underestimated how revolutionary his creation was. Bitcoin did not begin to catch on out of fun or convenience... It caught on out of necessity.

You see, bitcoin had no monetary value when it launched in January 2009. Bitcoin gradually gained value over the next four years. One bitcoin was worth $34 by March 1, 2013.

And then something happened on March 26, 2013, that changed the course of human history...

"All insured deposits (individuals and legal entities) up to €100,000 have, as of 26 March 2013, been transferred from Laiki Bank to the Bank of Cyprus," read an announcement from the Cyprus government...

> In addition, the entire amount of deposits belonging to financial institutions, the government, municipalities, municipal councils and other public entities, insurance companies, charities, schools, educational institutions, and deposits belonging to JCC Payment Systems Ltd have been transferred to the Bank of Cyprus.

The Bank of Cyprus then proceeded to charge a "levy" of 9.9% on all bank accounts over €100,000 as well as a levy of 6.75% on all bank accounts under €100,000. And they limited all ATM withdrawals to €400 a day.

In other words, they locked everybody's money inside the banking system so they could confiscate a portion of it to "bail-in" their failed banking system.

People rushed to ATMs to try to get their money out... so the withdrawal limit was decreased to €100. Still, the ATMs ran out of money very quickly. And nobody bothered to replenish them.

Average people watched helplessly as their money was frozen for a month. When they finally had access to their money once again, they found that there were now very strict rules regarding how much money they could take out of their bank accounts and what they could do with it. Capital controls became their reality.

Meanwhile, the price of bitcoin shot up 299% to $139 per bitcoin by April 30, 2013. People were beginning to realize that bitcoin was a way out... a safe haven.

Bitcoin went parabolic once that realization took hold. The price shot up another 727% to $1,151 per bitcoin by December 4, 2013.

But then it cooled back off as the situation in Cyprus settled down. In fact, bitcoin spent nearly two years cooling down as the macroeconomic climate remained quiet.

That is, until it happened again... this time in Greece.

Rumors suggesting that the Greek banking system was in trouble were circulating throughout the country in the early months of 2015. People were getting nervous.

On June 27, 2015, Panos Kammenos, head of the government's coalition ally in Greece, appeared on local television. "Citizens should not be scared, there is no blackmail," Kammenos assured the Greek people. "The banks won't shut, the ATMs will (have cash). All this is exaggeration."

The very next day, Greek Prime Minister Alexis Tsipras announced that banks in Greece would not open on Monday. "In the coming days, what's needed is patience and composure," Tsipras proclaimed. "The bank deposits of the Greek people are fully secure."

The government of Greece released the following guidance:

- From June 29, 2015, banks will remain closed up to and including July 6.

- Deposits are fully safeguarded.

- The payment of pensions is exempted from the restrictions on banking transactions.

- Electronic transactions within the country won't be affected. All transactions with credit or debit cards and other electronic forms (web banking, phone banking) can be conducted as normal.

- Prepaid cards may be used to the limit existing before the beginning of the bank holiday.

- **From midday June 29, ATMs will operate with a daily cash withdrawal limit of €60 per card, which is equivalent to €1,800 a month.**

- Foreign tourists can make cash withdrawals from ATMs with their cards without restrictions provided these have been issued abroad.

- Wages paid electronically to bank accounts aren't affected.

Instead of heeding the prime minister's call for patience, people stormed the ATMs, gas stations, and grocery stores. Lines went on for blocks.

The ATMs ran out of cash. The gas pumps ran dry. Food disappeared from store shelves.

The Greek people were no fools... They had seen this before. Cyprus was only 500 miles away, after all.

As it turns out, banks in Greece were closed for nearly a full month—leaving people with little access to their money.

And once again, bitcoin spiked in price as people fled the banking system looking for a safe place to store their money. Bitcoin gained another 206% over the course of the next year.

But this time, it did not cool back off. Nor did the macroeconomic climate remain quiet.

Instead, one event after another has driven more and more people to bitcoin... most looking for a safe place to store their wealth. Take a look at this chart:

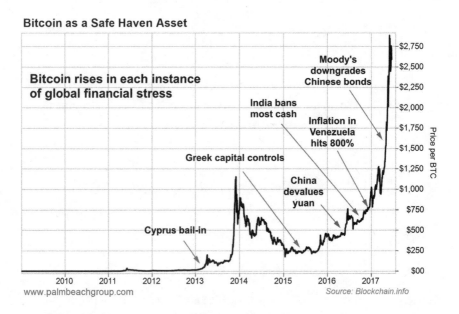

Far from being a cheap way to pay for games, as Satoshi originally suggested, bitcoin quickly became the world's prominent safe-haven asset. The more governments and big banks moved to control their money, the more people flocked to bitcoin as a solution.

In 2016, the People's Bank of China devalued the yuan, reducing its purchasing power significantly. Then India banned more than 80% of all cash in circulation... then inflation in Venezuela hit 800%... then Moody's downgraded Chinese bonds.

More and more people flooded into bitcoin with each incident, and its price exploded up to nearly $3,000 per bitcoin.

This crazy experiment with "internet money" was worthless in 2009. Less than a decade later, it was worth nearly 3,000 times more than the world's global reserve currency.

That's a story for the history books, if there ever was one.

So, the question now is: Will it last? Will bitcoin continue to attract more and more people until it becomes recognized as a legitimate payment network on a global scale?

Or is it just another iteration of the dot-com bubble that crashed and burned in 2000?

After all, the bitcoin network is terribly slow by global standards. As this book is being written, the bitcoin network can only process three to seven transactions per second. A scaling upgrade was recently approved, but even then, the network will only be able to handle 12–28 transactions per second.

Visa, on the other hand, processes 2,000 transactions per second. That puts bitcoin way behind the eight ball in terms of global adoption.

But to determine whether bitcoin's rise will last, you can't get caught up on where the network is today. You must look to the future.

You see, bitcoin is still in its infancy. It is a baby. The bitcoin you see today is not the final product.

To understand this, you need to understand that bitcoin is fundamentally a disruptive technology.

The Nature of Disruptive Technology

The thing about disruptive technology is that it always has to prove itself on outdated infrastructure designed specifically for the technology it seeks to disrupt.

Think about the first cars.

They had to demonstrate their value on dirt roads made specifically for horses.

This same dynamic was true of the internet. It first had to operate through the phone system, which was designed to carry human voices, not data.

That's where bitcoin is today.

Bitcoin is currently operating within the constructs of the legacy financial system.

This system is centralized and slow by design. It is a system of controls and surveillance. It was designed specifically to give a few people complete control over money and banking.

Bitcoin is awkward within this system because it is decentralized by design. It is peer-to-peer. It's open and transparent.

Bitcoin doesn't just give users control over their bank accounts. It makes everyone the president and CEO of their own bank.

But bitcoin still has to move in and out of the existing system to be fully functional right now. It's the car stuck on the dirt road. It's the weird noises coming from that thing called a "modem."

Disruptive technology is always awkward at first. Old people ignore it. Academics laugh at it. The media says it's for criminals.

But if the technology is useful enough, people gradually gravitate to it. Usually, they come from the fringes at first.

With user adoption comes development and innovation.

The development and innovation gradually attract more users. Which gradually spurs more development and innovation.

Then, one day, you wake up and the world has changed.

There are paved roads and cars everywhere. The horses are back on the farm.

But now there are also motorcycles. And bicycles. And skateboards. And Teslas.

These are the "apps" that were developed once the technology became mainstream.

The apps piggyback on the work done by the disruptive technology. They don't change the world—they make it wealthier and more interesting. But they could not come into existence until there was a market for them.

The disruptive technology is what creates the market.

Nobody was on the internet 30 years ago. The world-wide web wasn't invented until 1989. Netscape wasn't released until 1994.

People spend all their time on the internet today. They send 2.5 million emails every single second. They do video chats with each other. They are buried in Facebook. They gobble up shares of Snapchat's IPO.

The internet began as a quirky novelty. Now, human civilization would collapse if something happened to it.

What's funny about this is people always say that it happened overnight.

Video chats. Digital money. Immersive 3D worlds. Virtual reality.

These things were just science fiction when I was a kid. Nobody saw them coming.

That's because nobody was paying attention until they had no other choice.

The majority of people never see the genius and the struggle behind disruptive technology. They just see the end result when it becomes useful to them.

They become the market.

But that only happens after tons of blood, sweat, tears, and capital has poured into development and innovation.

As this book is being written, institutional money is beginning to flow into bitcoin... big money.

There was a Consensus Conference on bitcoin held in New York City in May 2017. For the first time in bitcoin's history, this conference wasn't an echo chamber for tech geeks, software developers, and sound-money libertarians. Instead, the conference was crawling with hedge fund managers... excited hedge fund managers.

Albert Wenger of Union Square Ventures said at the conference: "When we look back at the crypto space, and its $80 billion [value] right now, it will look like a small blip."

And here is Brian Kelly, BKCM hedge fund manager:

> *Six months ago, we started getting interest from family offices. Now we're getting interest from venture capitalists and small institutions. In three to five years, we'll be getting interest from pension funds. We are still in the first innings. I would use any price pullback to buy; there is a wall of money coming. Just 1% of institutional money and we would see an explosion in prices.*

Michael Moro of Genesis Global Trading added: "In the last six weeks, we've gone from millionaire conversations to billionaire conversations. There's plenty of money left to be deployed."

This "wall of money" is going to be used to fund bitcoin's expansion. The platform is going to scale, and it is going to become much more user friendly.

Ultimately, bitcoin is going to get to the point where you use it as effortlessly as you use your credit card today.

So, I think I will wake up one morning to learn that bitcoin has been an overnight success.

It will be a miracle. Nobody will have seen it coming. And when that day comes, today's adopters will become very wealthy.

I know this is a lot to chew on. But I felt like you needed to know the "why" before the "what" and the "how" would make sense.

So, let's take a step back for a minute.

Bitcoin is classified as a "cryptocurrency." It is the first of its kind, but bitcoin has spawned hundreds of other cryptocurrencies—each with unique properties and use cases. Next, we will dive a little deeper into cryptocurrencies...

Chapter 3:
Introducing Cryptocurrencies

High up in the mountains of Tibet lies a secret base.

An underused hydroelectric power plant sends an almost endless source of cheap energy to a remote mining base.

Industrious entrepreneurs use this cheap, abundant energy to mine millions of dollars' worth of a valuable new commodity.

But this is no ordinary mine...

There are no picks and shovels. Instead of shafts, miners work in rooms lined with endless rows of computers. Thousands of roaring fans keep the "mine" from overheating.

Every month, the mining operation produces millions of dollars in a new type of commodity.

The mine doesn't produce gold or any other precious metals...

Instead, it produces cryptocurrencies, including the world's most popular one: Bitcoin. And the industry is booming.

The owner of the mine is a 30-year-old whiz kid named Chandler Guo. At first glance, Guo seems like any other ordinary computer scientist. But he's much more than that. Bitcoin has made Guo rich. According to Guo, his operation mines 200 bitcoins per day. At market prices as of this writing, Guo is grossing $500,000 *per day*.

His total operation (including the base in Tibet) is now the third-largest bitcoin mining group in the world.

I had been reading about Guo for years... but could never get a meeting with him. I finally tracked him down in the East End of London. I was there to attend a blockchain conference, and Guo was one of the speakers.

I learned from Guo during my interview that he's thoroughly focused on bitcoin. In fact, Guo believes so strongly in bitcoin that he sells all other cryptocurrencies he mines at the base so he can buy more bitcoins. He told me, "In the digital world in the future, they will be using Bitcoin."

It's too good an opportunity. In his own words, he said, "At $700 a coin, bitcoin is too cheap. In 20 years, bitcoin will be a global [currency]. One bitcoin will be worth $1 million."

I know that might sound crazy, but there are only 11 million bitcoins left out of the 16 million that have been mined. By Guo's estimation, 5 million bitcoins have been lost (through owner deaths, hardware breakdowns, negligence, etc.). This backs up what I was told from another bitcoin millionaire, Jered Kenna. He thinks about one-third of all bitcoins have been irretrievably lost.

So, at $1 million per coin and with only 11 million available coins, Guo is anticipating that bitcoin will have a total worth of $11 trillion. Another bitcoin millionaire, Roger Ver, aka "Bitcoin Jesus," thinks bitcoin will be worth $500,000 per coin. That would give bitcoin a value of $5.5 trillion.

I know these numbers sound crazy. But if bitcoin becomes the equivalent of digital gold, these numbers aren't as nuts as they appear...

Consider that today, the total value of all mined gold in the world is $7 trillion. So, a case can be made that if Bitcoin *does* become a globally recognized asset class, you could see a price between $500,000 and $1 million per coin.

I've been bullish on bitcoin since 2015.

It's a perfect asymmetrical bet: It has vast upside, but the downside is limited.

So, yes, I'm a big fan.

But as much as I admire guys like Guo, I think they're missing the forest for the trees when it comes to cryptocurrencies.

The truth is: Bitcoin is just part of a much, much bigger picture.

In my conversations with the investing public and bitcoin experts, their entire focus is on replacing fiat (paper) money with digital money. I believe this will inevitably happen, but there is much more to this story than just money.

But before we begin exploring the vast use-cases for bitcoin—and the hundreds of cryptocurrencies it spawned—we need to lay some groundwork.

What Exactly Are Cryptocurrencies?

Money is one of the most confounding concepts on earth. We all use it. But who really understands it?

The truth is: *Money can be anything.*

In the past, seashells, salt, rice, barley—even silk—have been used as money. In essence, all you need is something that makes it easier for people to transact business between each other.

Take the U.S. dollar. There's nothing backing it up—we went off the gold standard in 1971. So, all the dollar really is *is a promise... an "act of faith."*

We're all acting on faith that by accepting these small pieces of paper we call "money," we'll, in turn, be able to use them to buy other stuff in the future.

A cryptocurrency, sometimes called "digital currency," is no different. It's simply internet-based money. And like any other medium of exchange, many people around the world have decided it is money.

They believe they'll be able to use cryptocurrency in the future to buy other stuff with it. *That* alone makes it have value.

How Do Cryptocurrencies Work?

This is where it's easy to get lost in the weeds.

To me, the best way to think about it is like this: We all drive cars, but how many of us understand the finer details of how an engine works?

As we discussed earlier, cryptocurrencies work thanks to something called a "blockchain," which is nothing more than a very secure online database. Just think of it as a public ledger.

In short, a cryptocurrency is a digital currency that uses cryptography to secure transactions and create new units.

Cryptocurrencies are basically computer codes that can be used to transfer things of value. These transactions take place over the blockchain, which is essentially a public ledger.

It's not that much different than when one bank sends money to another. They use ledgers to track the transactions. The difference, as we've mentioned before, is the blockchain is a decentralized ledger. So, the transaction is tracked over multiple computers.

Some cryptocurrencies, like bitcoin, are used as money (a medium of exchange). Others are similar to equities or stocks (will go over that in a later chapter).

The main difference between cryptocurrencies and traditional currencies is that the cryptocurrencies are digital and use cryptography.

A Groundbreaking New Way to Make Transactions

We live in a modern age with all types of new technologies. But did you know we're still using antiquated methods to make payments? And it's costing us billions per year.

You see, during Roman times, bankers would transfer money via what we'd consider today as paper checks.

According to a Goldman Sachs report, paper checks still make up 50% of all business payments. So, we're sending $26 trillion per year through a system that was invented 2,000 years ago.

The cost of this antiquated approach is mammoth.

All-in costs surrounding these outdated payment systems are estimated at $550 billion per year.

To put that in perspective, that amount is 3.5-times bigger than all the profits made by U.S. banks in 2014. It's twice the size of the global PC market... and almost as big as the annual Pentagon budget.

So, what are the problems with the way we handle money as a society now?

For one, it's inefficient. It takes days to verify transactions, and mistakes are made in the process.

Second, money can be counterfeited. According to the Secret Service, about $300 million in fake U.S. currency is removed from circulation each year. And that doesn't include check forgeries and credit card fraud.

Cryptocurrencies solve these two major problems using the blockchain.

Let me explain how it works...

When you go to the bank and withdraw money, the teller checks the bank's electronic ledger to see your balance.

Once the teller sees that you have enough money to withdraw, he or she gives you your money and changes the ledger to reflect the withdrawal.

If you immediately go to an ATM at a different bank, you'll see that the ledger has already been shared with the other bank.

This is called a closed-ledger system. Only other banks and payment networks can view this ledger.

The blockchain works similarly, but the ledger is public and online. Identities are kept anonymous, but all transaction details can be seen by everyone.

The blockchain is maintained by thousands of independent computers across the world. These computers are constantly "talking" to one another, comparing data to make sure the ledger is valid.

This prevents double spending the same way banks prevent double spending.

Even better, the blockchain is unhackable and impossible to shut down because there's no central server. Being unhackable means no one can tamper with the information on the blockchain.

And because the blockchain uses cryptology (a secure form of communication), it's also difficult to counterfeit cryptocurrencies.

So, this creates trust without needing a central authority or middleman. When you cut out middlemen, you cut out lots of costs. This is already changing the face of the money-transmitting business.

For example, you can now send money in any currency to any place in the world that has an internet connection for 99.9% less than it costs to send money by Western Union. The recipient will receive the money immediately.

Paying 5–10% of the money you send in a wire transfer and waiting seven days for that money to clear will be things of the past.

In a few years, you'll be able to buy a home without having to spend $3,000 on title insurance. The blockchain can do that in seconds.

Two Trillion Reasons (and Counting) Why Blockchain Is the Future

In a recent report, *Forbes* estimated that cybercrime costs are expected to reach $2 trillion by 2019. By moving much of our existing technology architecture from a centralized to a decentralized model, such as the blockchain, cybercrime as we know it can be virtually eliminated.

The potential savings and future profit opportunities promised by blockchain technology is why I believe many fortunes in this space will be made from the underlying blockchain technology itself.

If you look at the banking sector, industry giants like JPMorgan Chase, Barclays, and the Royal Bank of Scotland (among many others) are pouring billions of dollars into developing financial applications that use blockchain technology.

JPMorgan alone publicly announced that it will invest $9 billion in blockchain technology.

This movement to the blockchain is all about money. A blockchain-based financial system can virtually eliminate fraud, delays in payment, and trade errors. Hundreds of billions of dollars are at stake... and that's just in the banking sector.

Many try to explain the blockchain in terms of the "new internet." I'll admit: Even I'm guilty of that. The problem with this analogy is that we're using old technology in an attempt to define an entirely new paradigm.

Much like the dawn of the Internet Age, we don't even have the lexicon yet to explain the coming era. Even as I write this, I struggle to find the words to explain it—it's that cutting edge.

But it is important to understand that the blockchain is not only about money and payments. Which brings us to the world's second most valuable cryptocurrency: Ethereum.

Chapter 4:
Vitalik Buterin and the Ethereum Revolution

He's been called autistic, a prodigy, and even the next Steve Jobs.

But whatever he is, Vitalik Buterin, a Canadian programmer now living in Switzerland, will go down in history as a revolutionary figure.

You see, Vitalik Buterin isn't your average millennial.

In 2011, Vitalik became the co-founder of *Bitcoin Magazine*—the first publication dedicated to covering the groundbreaking new technology. He also served as the publication's leading writer.

In 2013, he took a page out of the Steve Jobs playbook and dropped out of college.

One year later, he won a $100,000 fellowship from billionaire PayPal co-founder, Peter Thiel. Then, he went on to win a "World Technology Award," beating out Facebook's Mark Zuckerberg.

Then, in 2015, Vitalik released an innovative new cryptocurrency called Ethereum.

Ethereum is its own ecosystem like its more famous brother, bitcoin. But there are differences between the two.

For one, Ethereum is a development platform that people can build upon. It's similar to the operating system developed by Apple (called iOS) to run apps on its products.

The Ethereum network is also much faster than bitcoin's. It will process and confirm a transaction within 15 seconds. It takes 10 minutes for bitcoin.

Finally, the network design is different from bitcoin. It's designed for developers to build upon, but with a unique angle: Any program built on the Ethereum network must spend ether (the currency) for it to run.

This does two things:

- It prevents malicious or non-productive use of the Ethereum system.

- The more the system is used, the more demand it creates for ether.

So basically, the value of ether is based on the law of supply and demand. The more the system is used, the more demand for the currency is generated. That's exactly how currencies are supposed to work—demand and use drives price.

Like bitcoin, Ethereum is a decentralized platform that runs smart contracts. Decentralized applications are called "DApps" for short.

Each DApp runs exactly as programmed, without any possibility of downtime, censorship, fraud, or third-party interference.

These applications run on a custom-built blockchain. The blockchain is a shared network that can move value around and represent property ownership.

Smart contracts are only executed when prespecified conditions are met. And the blockchain automatically enforces the terms of the agreement.

Let me give you an example...

Today, if you wanted to sell your house, it would require a lot of paperwork, legal agreements, and fees. It's a slow and expensive process.

Ethereum's goal is to turn that lengthy process into a digital transaction recognized and verified by the blockchain.

That would make the transaction faster and more secure. Third parties wouldn't have to get involved. And it would save significant transaction fees.

This is just one type of transaction. The possibilities are limitless. Ethereum will do for any programmable products what bitcoin did for money and currency.

Some people believe Ethereum could spell the end of bureaucracy, creating trust and transparency among governments, institutions, corporations, and individuals.

And it will be as easy as sending an email.

As more developers build more DApps for the Ethereum network, the price of ether will rise higher.

Unlike bitcoin, the Ethereum network has garnered serious interest from major institutions.

Wells Fargo, Barclays, BMO, Credit Suisse, Natixis, HSBC, TD Bank, RBS, UBS, Unicredit, and the Commonwealth Bank of Australia have all given it a try.

And another 31 banks, including JPMorgan Chase, Bank of America, and Citibank, are looking into it.

"This is a very exciting development," said David Rutter, the man in charge of the blockchain for banking consortium, R3.

Tech giants have also joined in, with IBM, Samsung, and Microsoft all recently setting up partnerships with Ethereum founder, Vitalik Buterin.

According to Marley Gray, director of Microsoft's Azure project, a big reason companies are choosing Buterin's technology is because it's 40 times faster than bitcoin.

40 times faster.

What does that mean?

Well, say you want to cash in a check at a bank.

As you know, it can take anywhere from three to five days for that check to clear.

That's because of the way our current banking system is set up.

It's essentially using "old plumbing."

With digital currencies, however, it doesn't take nearly as long for money to clear. For bitcoin, it takes 10 minutes.

But with Buterin's new currency, the same transaction takes less than 15 seconds.

It's almost instantaneous.

That's why everyone is jumping all over this. Speed is king. And for these billion-dollar companies, minutes matter.

In fact, even the $2 trillion Toronto Stock Exchange is looking into Buterin's currency.

"It's exciting," says Anthony Di Iorio, the exchange's chief digital officer.

Google has been tracking Ethereum for quite some time now. And just recently, one of its algorithms indicated a major spike in the currency's popularity. So I flew to Austin, Texas, to find out what was going on.

Caterina Rindo, a top consultant in the digital currency space, was presenting at the SXSW (South by Southwest) conference.

Rindo told me there's been a major shift toward Ethereum in the tech community.

In May 2016, I attended another major cryptocurrency conference in New York called Consensus.

During the conference, I spoke to at least 20 people per day. From bank executives to some of the world's top information and technology officers.

Every one of them was in the process of testing Buterin's system. I heard terms like "revolutionary" and "this could save us billions" applied to his technology.

In fact, at a recent New York City "hackathon" (this is where many of the world's best programmers compete on new technologies), 86% of programmers chose to work on Buterin's new currency over bitcoin.

You see, a large part of a new technology's success has to do with the early adopters and developers.

Take Apple, for example.

The company wouldn't be anywhere near where it is today if it hadn't been for hordes of diehard fans and developers—*many of whom worked for free*—who improved the technology over the years.

Buterin, like Jobs, is quickly developing a "cult-like" following. (At the conference where I met him, he was mobbed by hordes of fans.)

In fact, even though he only started his project in late 2014, more than 38,779 individuals around the world quickly signed up to attend local workshops to learn more about—and help support—Ethereum.

The Benefits of Ethereum's Blockchain

Before he created the Ethereum network, Buterin wrote for *Bitcoin Magazine*. And although he still owns bitcoin, he recognized some weaknesses with it that he wanted to improve.

So, what was the novel improvement Buterin made to bitcoin?

You see, bitcoin is essentially a payment system. And it uses the blockchain to register those transactions.

That's where Buterin's big idea came in and why so many banks are interested in his network.

He recognized that if you could make payment transactions using blockchain software, you could make *any* type of transaction if you wrote the proper code.

And that's what Buterin did with Ethereum. He created a program that could create "customized" transactions based on each developer's needs.

In other words, you could write real estate and insurance contracts, mortgages, and even stock purchases using Ethereum—all without a middleman (or lawyer!).

And that's one reason Ethereum is distinctly different from bitcoin.

No wonder he won a prestigious World Technology Award for his invention. And it's also no wonder some of the biggest venture capitalists in the world are getting behind Ethereum.

Two other areas Buterin wanted to improve were speed and security.

As previously mentioned, it takes 10 minutes to process a single transaction on the Bitcoin network. Ethereum takes 15 seconds. That's 40 times faster. And within five years, Buterin expects to get that number down to one to four seconds.

Now, compare that to paying for something with a check or even a debit card. The transaction could take days to clear your account.

And because every digital currency transaction is encrypted and verified on the blockchain, counterfeiting is nearly impossible.

Now, compare that to other forms of money.

According to some estimates, more than $1 billion in fake checks are passed off in the United States per year. And the toll is more than $8 billion in credit card fraud.

But Ethereum will do more than make moving *money* safer and faster. It will make *all types of business transactions* safer and faster.

You see, bitcoin was designed solely for payments. It was never designed to handle massive amounts of complicated transactions.

Buterin's solution is more than just a new currency or payment system, though.

It's an operating system that supports complex computer programs. Other developers can build software applications on Ethereum to fix payment problems and inefficiencies.

Big banks are spending close to $1 billion per year testing this new technology. Virtually all of them are testing Ethereum.

Why are the banks picking Ethereum?

Because Ethereum promises to smooth out these transaction problems and bring payment-processing costs down to 1/100 of a penny. That means these giant corporations could save billions of dollars by adopting the blockchain.

That's why Ethereum holds the promise of a whole new way to conduct global business.

Why Businesses Will Choose Ethereum

Ethereum is an operating system like Android or Microsoft Windows. Developers write programs that run on the Ethereum system in much the same way they do for Windows or for apps that run on Android phones.

Ethereum is different because it's an operating system for the blockchain. So, instead of having to create your own blockchain, you can build programs on top of Ethereum's blockchain.

This makes rolling out a blockchain application much faster and cheaper than building an entire blockchain network from scratch.

That's why banks, brokers, insurance companies, and exchange officials are so excited about Ethereum. They don't have to invest in a vast network of distributed computers.

They also don't have to create their own programming language.

All they have to do is build whatever application they want and run it on the Ethereum network.

The beauty of it all is... anytime Buterin's Ethereum technology is used, the currency attached to the Ethereum network has to be used... so it creates a natural demand for ether.

And that demand drives up the price of ether.

This was done to make it very expensive for hackers to upload malicious code to the Ethereum blockchain and for spammers to overwhelm it. The currency also ensures that the blockchain will be used for generating value.

You see, miners receive ether in exchange for verifying transactions. Think of it as an incentive to keep the network as decentralized as possible.

It's my belief that the Ethereum network will become the global operating standard for virtually all blockchain applications in the same way that Windows became the global operating standard for personal computers.

As the system catches on, more people will use ether to conduct transactions. And this will boost its price.

And guess what? Microsoft is doing a lot of work on Ethereum.

On March 30, 2016, Microsoft announced that more than 3 million of its developers would have access to work on Ethereum through its Windows platform.

This is huge.

You see, Ethereum is developing a "cult-like" following among the tech savvy... just like many "techies" did for Steve Jobs and his Apple products.

But don't make the mistake of thinking it's too late to get in... there's still plenty of meat left on this bone. Remember, bitcoin went from pennies to $17, then exploded all the way up to $3,000.

So, there's a lot more room to go in Ethereum.

In fact, one emerging buyer is Wall Street...

According to *The New York Times*, Michael Novogratz, who managed $2.3 billion at Fortress Investment Group, has just made a "significant" purchase. We expect many more as Ethereum starts to go mainstream.

Remember, Ethereum is only two years old, and it already has the world's largest banks and software companies lining up to work on it. Ethereum is the second-largest cryptocurrency in the world.

As of this writing, very few outside of the tech world know about the ether currency and the Ethereum network. It's barely hit the mainstream news yet. It hasn't been on *60 Minutes*, and it's still relatively unknown.

We will talk about all the different uses for the Ethereum network and blockchain technology later in the book.

But before we dive into the specifics, we need to zoom back out and look at the big picture again, given what we now know.

Chapter 5:
How Blockchain Will Change the World

Here's what we know...

The blockchain was initially developed in 2008 as an online network to track Bitcoin payments.

Each transaction record is called a block. A block is essentially a line of computer code. Each block of code is programmed to accept Bitcoin as payment. After a block is verified, it's added to the chain of previous blocks—hence the name.

Think of it as a bookkeeper adding entries into a ledger—except this "ledger" is public and online.

The blockchain is maintained by thousands of independent computers. These computers constantly "talk" to each other and compare data to make sure the ledger is valid.

Each individual computer connected to the network (called a node) must verify a transaction before it's added to the chain. By storing data across its network, the blockchain eliminates many of the risks that come with storing data in a central location.

Think of it this way... Security concerns being equal, it's more efficient for criminals to rob one giant central bank than thousands of individual small banks. Even if the smaller banks are less secure, crooks would have to break into hundreds or thousands of them to steal the equivalent of the motherlode they'd pocket if they could break into a more secure central bank.

Got it? Good.

Now here's what we're learning...

As it turns out, blockchain technology can do much more than track Bitcoin payments. In fact, the blockchain is going to radically disrupt the way traditional commerce and industry has operated for at least one hundred years now.

By the way, we aren't talking 10 or 20 years down the road. We are talking *right now*.

This chapter will go over the areas where blockchain technology will have the biggest impact. Keep in mind, many of these functions are already in development. Others are more theoretical at the moment.

How to Liberate Trillions in "Dead Capital"

One of the most important social mechanisms in the developed world is the institution of private property and the accompanying systems for titling land and real estate.

Private property is the foundation of commerce, yet a huge swath of economic activity occurs in places where no effective system for titling property exists.

Here's why this is important: There is major misconception surrounding the "third world."

Third world countries, and their inhabitants, are relatively poor—that's easy for us to see. What we fail to see is why they are poor.

The misconception is that they are poor because they don't have money. So, first world nations send over $100 billion in foreign aid to the third world every single year.

And it doesn't do one bit of good. Hundreds of billions of dollars later, the third world remains poor.

This may surprise you, but you can visit third world nations and stay in an established hotel with a brand that you recognize.

When you step outside of those hotels, you are not leaving behind the internet, television programming, and modern medicine. The third world has access to those things, at least to a certain degree.

What you are really leaving behind is the institution of private property, and the legal infrastructure for titling, registering, and enforcing property rights.

That is why third world nations are poor. They are buried in what economist Hernando de Soto called "dead capital."

You see, third world residents have real estate... but their ownership of it is tenuous at best. Their home provides a roof over their head, but that's it.

They can't easily sell their real estate. They can't use it as collateral to access credit for productive purposes. Under those circumstances, there's very little incentive to improve or even maintain the property.

Compare this to the Unites States where total real estate transactions total hundreds of billions of dollars every single year. That's hundreds of billions of dollars moving around in the economy for all kinds of different purposes.

Sure, some of that money may be squandered. But much of it is used as capital for productive purposes like starting or expanding a business, investing in a promising company, putting solar panels on the roof, or even just general home improvements.

So, you see, the third world has assets. But without a formal system of property rights, it doesn't have the means of converting those assets into productive capital.

Here's how de Soto put it:

> *With titles, shares and property laws, people could suddenly go beyond looking at their assets as they are—houses used for shelter—to thinking about what they could be—things like security for credit to start or expand a business.*

In fact, the Institute for Liberty and Democracy (ILD) estimates that there is nearly $10 trillion in dead capital stuck in developing nations without a formal system of property rights.

That is about to change.

Blockchain technology will be used to create a global standard for titling land and real estate. There are several blockchain companies already working on this functionality with San Francisco-based BitFury being the most prominent.

As of this writing, BitFury (a blockchain tech company) is working directly with the Republic of Georgia to title and register the nation's property on the blockchain. Once complete, this system will eliminate the need for bureaucracies, courts, and middle-men and drastically cut costs.

The process of bringing blockchain land-titling services to every nation in the world will be a tedious one. But it will happen.

Inevitably there will be certain nations that resist blockchain-based property rights at first. But the resistors will be forced to participate when they see the explosion of economic activity, innovation, and prosperity that follows the liberation of dead capital.

Even in the developed world, the process for obtaining proper deeds and titles is subject to centralization and counterparties which brings with it fees, costs, and taxes that skim off every transaction.

That's all going to come to an end as well.

The blockchain will provide cheap access to a land titling system for billions of people around the world which will inevitably drive commerce, spur production, and create wealth in places where very little currently exists.

Chapter 6:
The Blockchain Will Conquer Wall Street

Patrick Byrne is the CEO of Overstock.com, the American online retailer. He gave the keynote speech at the Mises Institute's Austrian Economics Research Conference in 2015.

In his talk, Patrick asked the audience members to raise their hands if they owned any stock... many hands went up.

"Every single one of you with your hand up is incorrect—none of you own any stock. That's not how the system works."

Patrick went on to explain how the system of securities settlement in the U.S. has divorced the transfer of money from the transfer of securities.

Anyone invested in the stock market has a broker—either full-service or discount online broker—who handles settlement for them. Most people think that these brokers move money and securities around between the accounts of buyers and sellers. Indeed, that's how the system did work prior to 1973. Back then, brokers would transfer physical stock certificates and keep real-time ownership records.

Everything changed in 1973 with the creation of The Depository Trust & Clearing Corporation (DTCC). Settlement for securities transactions in the U.S. is now centralized within the DTCC, and all brokers involved in U.S. financial markets are plumbed into this private organization.

So, money and securities do not actually move between the accounts of buyers and sellers. They move between accounts housed centrally within the DTCC.

But the system takes centralization one step further.

U.S. stocks are registered in the name of an organization called Cede & Co., which is a subsidiary of the DTCC. This means that Cede & Co. is the legal owner of the vast majority of all U.S. equities.

Unless you take the necessary steps to register a stock in your name, you do not technically own it. What you own is a contractual right, or I.O.U., to that stock.

Actually, it is even more complicated than that.

Because there are several layers of counterparties, you really own a contractual right (your broker) to a contractual right (DTCC) to a contractual right (Cede & Co.) of the stock that appears in your brokerage account.

Now, this system was set-up during a time when records were not kept in computer databases, but on pieces of paper in filing cabinets. Record keeping in the financial markets had become extremely costly, inefficient, and problematic. This was back in the '70s when mainframe computing was still choice technology.

Regardless of intent, this system deliberately separates investors from their ownership rights. Not to mention, this system is extremely inefficient and fragile, as it is based upon 40-year-old technology.

Well guess what?

Securities settlement—both in the equity markets and the credit markets—is a fantastic application for blockchain technology.

The blockchain can return securities ownership directly to investors and enable peer-to-peer settlement in which the buyer sends money directly to the seller, who delivers the security directly to the buyer. Peer-to-peer settlement on the blockchain renders high-frequency trading, front-running, and market manipulation nearly impossible.

Sounds pretty good, right?

Here's the kicker—if you move the financial markets onto the blockchain, then you cut 90% of Wall Street out of the picture entirely. And you make the U.S. Securities and Exchange Commission (SEC), Financial Industry Regulatory Authority (FINRA), and most of the financial regulatory apparatus obsolete. There's nothing for them to regulate because the blockchain cannot be gamed or corrupted.

If you cut out these intermediaries, then you also cut out most of the commissions, fees, taxes, and overhead cost associated with the financial markets. These costs are relatively minor for each individual transaction, but the cumulative total is gargantuan.

The DTCC settles nearly **$2 quadrillion** in value every single year.

Even if total settlement costs, including taxes, average five basis points per transaction (0.05%), we are still talking about more than $1 trillion in cumulative commissions, fees, and taxes being sucked away by Wall Street and government's regulatory complex.

Imagine what the world looks like if that $1 trillion worth of investable capital is left in the economy! You would witness an economic boom unprecedented before in human history.

It is coming...

Chapter 7:
The Blockchain Will Solve the Welfare Crisis

The U.S. welfare system is in crisis.

The Heritage Foundation estimates that the U.S. government has spent $22 trillion on welfare alone since 1964.

Yet, there are more recipients today than ever before. More than 21% of Americans received some type of welfare in 2015, according to the U.S. Census Bureau. That's up from 18.6% in 2009.

The welfare state has not eliminated poverty... it has institutionalized it.

The welfare state model has been an utter failure for most people. But I don't mean to suggest that people should not help one another...

What's largely been forgotten is that mutual aid societies were widespread before the modern welfare state. A mutual aid society is an organization formed to provide financial support, networking, and/or insurance among its members.

Mutual aid societies were so large in the U.S. back in the early 20th century that many employed their own full-time doctors. They were called "lodge doctors" and served the needs of the society's members.

In other words, you didn't go to the hospital when you had a problem. You called the lodge doctor and he came to you. Of course, this did not preclude members from seeking medical care from hospitals or general practitioners. But their mutual-aid health coverage was more focused and more personal. And it didn't require an expensive government program.

In addition to basic welfare and insurance services, mutual aid societies also built orphanages, retirement homes, job exchanges, and even created scholarship programs.

Because membership dues were tied directly to mutual-aid expenses, all members had an incentive to keep their personal costs as low as possible. As the welfare state expanded, most of these mutual aid societies gradually disappeared. Not because the welfare state was better... but because it promised utopia without any costs.

Except there was no utopia. And the costs were enormous.

The government generally skims 50% off the top of the economy to support welfare states. That money is systematically filtered through layers of bureaucracy.

Very little is actually used to help people.

Let the people who earned their money keep it, and the global economy will boom like never before. This would eliminate the need for mandatory social welfare programs because people would have the resources to create their own mutual aid societies.

Don't believe me?

A colleague participated in a GoFundMe.com mutual-aid campaign for a young teenager who was tragically paralyzed. He didn't know the kid or his family, but the story found him on the Internet and he was touched by it. So, he kicked in $100 and wrote a nice note.

Do you know how much money this campaign raised for medical expenses?

Over $17,000—mostly in $10, $20, or $100 contributions from people who somehow came across the story online. By the way, this money was to cover deductibles and copays in addition to the catastrophic insurance coverage.

What's a government's disability check? 900 bucks a month? I'll take mutual aid any day.

Now, let's take this a step further.

You can build mutual aid "smart contracts" on the blockchain.

Smart contracts are self-executing contracts that use access to external data feeds and a cryptocurrency payment network to emulate the logic of contractual clauses. Here's how this would work:

Mutual-aid members would pay membership premiums into a cryptocurrency "pool" on the blockchain.

This pool of funds would be governed by a smart contract with very specific and agreed-upon rules regarding when the funds could be released. The rules would cover medical emergencies, car accidents, disability, maternity care, etc. Each mutual aid society would be free to determine its own coverage rules.

When a mutual-aid member experiences a covered event—like a car accident for example—there would be a process for verifying the damages on the blockchain. Once verified, the smart contract would release the approved funds to the member.

This would all be done automatically, according to a predetermined protocol. There would be no need for insurance adjusters, lawyers, government bureaucrats, or any other middlemen.

In this way, the blockchain is going to return welfare to private citizens and organizations... And in the process, it will disrupt the insurance industry, too.

This isn't going to happen all at once, but blockchain-based mutual aid alternatives will begin popping up as the welfare model falls into a state of fiscal chaos.

The beauty of the mutual aid model is that it's 100% voluntary. Individuals are free to join or shun mutual aid societies according to their own preferences. That's not the case with the welfare model in which everyone is required, by force, to support the system.

Further, blockchain technology makes it possible to spread mutual aid across borders. In the past, mutual aid was localized by necessity. The blockchain will enable global mutual-aid organizations, each with differing philosophies and coverage options.

And by cutting out the middlemen, blockchain-based mutual aid will also cut out the cronyism, inefficiency, and conflicting incentives that have plagued the modern welfare state for the past 100 years.

Chapter 8:
Global Trade Finance Has Not Changed in 400 Years... Until Now

On a cold and rainy October day in 1971, Ray Tomlinson sent the first ever email.

At the time, he didn't think much of it. Nobody told him to do it... He just thought it was neat.

Tomlinson was a programmer working on a secret government project called ARPANET... a network of computers that could "talk" to one another.

It took two years before people realized just how powerful Tomlinson's invention was. By then, email had gone from virtually none to 75% of all ARPANET traffic.

Today, 2.5 billion people send 2.5 million emails per second on ARPANET's successor—the internet.

More than four decades after Tomlinson's invention, email is still the single most used application on the internet. It was crucial to the growth of the web.

In the early days of the internet, email was its primary draw for users. There was no YouTube, Google, or iTunes Store.

Email birthed some of the earliest internet success stories... pioneering online service providers like Prodigy, CompuServe, and America Online that were all built on providing convenient email access.

Email was once a disruptive technology... Its use is so widespread that it's putting the U.S. Postal Service out of business... It's contributed to a 35% drop in first-class mail over the past decade.

Early investors in email support technology got rich, turning tiny investments into millions of dollars today.

It's easy for us to dream what it would have been like to make that sort of fortune from an investment. Had we the right information back in the 1980s and 1990s, would we have invested? Would we have committed those dollars?

Today, I'm putting your feet to the fire.

Friends, we are on the brink of a budding new technology trend that is of the same scale—possibly bigger—as email and the internet. But this one will revolutionize the way we transact and do business... in the way email revolutionized communication.

It's happening right now with only a few people watching...

Trade Finance Comes to the Blockchain

On September 7, 2016, Barclays facilitated a $100,000 trade of cheese and butter between Irish food company Ornua and the Seychelles Trading Company.

This small trade will be just as revolutionary as the first email sent.

Here's why...

When two companies in different countries want to buy and sell from each other, they use a bank to guarantee the transaction... It's called "trade finance."

According to McKinsey & Co., about $2 trillion is conducted in trade finance each year.

For more than 400 years, trade finance hasn't changed much. Banks act as intermediaries between trading partners. They use letters of credit to guarantee that everyone gets paid. Part of the due diligence process has always involved collecting a mass of paperwork.

Both sides have to prove they truly own what they say they own. They also have to prove that the goods they are selling are of the size, quality, and quantity that the bank is guaranteeing.

As you can imagine, trade finance involves sending mounds of paperwork across oceans. Missing a signature? Sorry, please resend the package. It's a time-consuming process desperately in need of change.

Even in today's digital age, it takes 10 days on average just to handle the paperwork. Sometimes, it can take up to a month.

But all of that just changed on September 7, 2016.

That $100,000 trade for butter and cheese was concluded in less than four hours. That's a huge time saver that will significantly reduce the price of international trade.

You already know how the deal was done... Barclays Bank used blockchain technology.

Remember, the blockchain is a digital ledger that is tamper-proof. No single party has the power to change the records. Instead of sitting in a single central location, the ledger "lives" on thousands of computers that automatically update.

The blockchain also has a built-in electronic record-keeping and transaction system. Both trade parties are able to track all documentation via a secure network. That means no third-party verification is required.

Barclays' global head of trade and working capital, Baihas Baghdadi, said that the blockchain will be a game changer.

> *We've proved the reality of this technology and the client Ornua has asked us when they can do the next transaction in this way, which proves how user-friendly the entire process was.*

Think about that for a second...

Trade finance hasn't changed since the 1600s. More than $2 trillion a year is conducted via trade finance and it's still done with bits of paper flying across the world's oceans.

The first ever trade deal done exclusively on the blockchain is as big as Ray Tomlinson's first email.

It's a whole new way for business to get done. In a few short years, most international trade will be conducted through a blockchain... just like most of the world's communications is done via email.

It's not every day you get to see a life-changing trend happen right before your eyes.

In a few short years, the word "blockchain" will be as commonplace as email. And it will spawn entire new industries.

Chapter 9:
Application Coins

When most people think about cryptocurrencies, their entire focus is on replacing paper money with digital money.

But there are so many other applications for cryptocurrencies and blockchain technology. This technology is going to disrupt literally every single industry in the world. A century's worth of traditions and standards is going to be replaced by radically superior methods... by "App Coins."

Application Coins or "App Coins" (also called digital tokens) are cryptocurrencies that serve a wide array of digital functions. They are used to make transactions on their respective blockchains.

For example, the ether token is used to make transactions on the Ethereum network. Each blockchain runs on its own cryptocurrency or digital token...

The currencies are "money" that can be spent or saved... but some tokens also act as "shares" for blockchain startups. In other words, they give you equity in a blockchain venture.

These shares are similar to buying stock in a traditional company. As more people use a particular blockchain, its "shares" increase in price... just like stocks do.

Finding the Next FANGs

Imagine if you could buy Facebook, Amazon, Netflix, or Google (the so-called FANG stocks) when they were startups. You'd be sitting on life-changing gains if you had...

But unlike most startups that require you to be an accredited investor (with a net worth of at least $1 million), anyone can buy "shares" in a blockchain startup. All you have to do is buy its app coin or token.

Today, most people view the blockchain simply as an online database (or digital ledger) that tracks bitcoin payments. But it's rapidly evolving beyond its original function as a platform for bitcoin transactions.

Soon, you'll be able to trade securities (stocks and bonds), sign contracts, buy and sell real estate, and even vote for presidents on new blockchain technologies.

In this chapter, I'll show you several sectors that the blockchain is poised to disrupt in the near future...

These new innovators are sidestepping the typical initial public offering (IPO). If they were traditional companies, they would almost surely still be private. You wouldn't have access to them... only venture capitalists and professional investors would.

But App Coins are offered to the public through "Initial Coin Offerings" or ICOs. And the best thing is that anyone can participate in an ICO. So, in this chapter, we are going to look at several prominent App Coins already in existence.

Buying Old Winners Won't Work

How do we make money from the blockchain revolution?

I can tell you: It won't be by buying into Facebook, Amazon, Netflix, or Google. The leaders of today rarely make the leap to become the leaders of tomorrow.

Think about IBM in the 1980s. It was a natural fit to dominate the burgeoning field of personal computers. Yet it was a spunky startup out of Redmond, Washington, called Microsoft that ended up eating IBM's lunch.

What about online shopping? Surely, in the 1990s, Wal-Mart should have dominated the shift to online shopping, right? But it didn't. A small startup called Amazon crushed Wal-Mart in the online space.

What about streaming video? If anybody should have had that market locked, it would have been Blockbuster, right? But by 2010, Netflix put it out of business.

The problem with entrenched players is that they are making so much money off the old model, they are loath to blow it up and embrace the new model. And that is why we must look at new companies if we want to grab a piece of the enormous upside ahead of us in the blockchain space.

There's a new breed of blockchain technology leader...

They want to do for the blockchain what Google did for search... what Apple did for phones... and what Facebook did for social media.

Let me explain...

The men and women creating these disruptive technologies are using a brand-new form of company.

Traditionally, innovators would create a private company... and then take it public through the IPO. As an investor, you could buy "shares" of the company and watch the share price grow.

These new innovators are doing much the same in the blockchain space with App Coins.

As I wrote earlier, App Coins are a way to invest in the growth of blockchain technology companies.

You can buy and sell these tokens on digital exchanges. The tokens give you direct equity ownership of the profit streams the network generates. We will go over how to do this later in the book.

This is a truly disruptive innovation. When companies can completely bypass the capital markets and "go public" by issuing cryptographic tokens that come with ownership/profit-sharing rights... it's an amazing innovation.

That is something we want to be part of.

Now, not every App Coin will be a smashing success. Many will fail in the marketplace and eventually go away.

But some of these will become the next FANG "stocks."

In the following pages, I'm going to go over a few examples of how App Coins will disrupt traditional industries.

The New Leader in Social Media

On February 4, 2004, while working from a nondescript dorm room in Harvard University, a baby-faced teenager changed the world. In a few short years, the social media leaders of the day—Myspace and Friendster—were all crushed under the heel of what was originally called "The Facebook."

Thirteen years later, Facebook is now worth over $437 billion. Today, Mark Zuckerberg, Facebook's CEO and founder, is one of America's richest men with a net worth over $55 billion.

And now, the same disruptive forces that propelled him to the top of America's wealthiest citizens are conspiring against him to completely remake the inner workings of social networks.

People spend hours each day adding to their Facebook "feeds" (like announcement boards)... feverishly hoping to amass "likes" from their friends, family, and even strangers. This has turned Facebook's users into unpaid and unwitting content creators.

What's smart about Facebook is the company matches "contextual" ads to the content created by users. So, if someone is sharing a post about a new sofa they bought, Facebook will place home furnishing ads next to the post.

What is brilliant about Zuckerberg is that by putting a thumbs up "like" button next to each post, he harnessed the human need to connect and be "liked" in a way no one before him had done. Zuckerberg transformed this deep human need for approval into a company that has the sixth-largest market capitalization in the world.

All social networks now follow Zuckerberg's model.

Twitter, Snapchat, Instagram, YouTube, and Reddit extract tens of billions of dollars in revenue from its users' content. With the exception of YouTube, none of that money ever trickles back down to the users of the system.

All the economic value is sucked up by the network and redistributed to shareholders of the various network providers. Since the early 2000s, this has been the model. It's been a brilliant piece of social engineering. The platform providers get the physical monetary value from the content... and the creators get an emotional token (the "like") in return.

So far, this system has worked exceedingly well... *for the platform providers*.

The users of the social networks of tomorrow will demand something more. They will want payment for the content they post.

The blockchain will make that happen.

Here's How the Blockchain Is Disrupting Social Networks

Whenever you don't have to invest hundreds of millions in computing power, you can scale your operation very quickly.

The blockchain is helping companies do just that.

With the emergence of blockchain technology, new companies have figured out how to use this cost advantage to rise quickly and displace Facebook, Snapchat, Instagram, Reddit, YouTube, and other dominant players.

Here's how they're doing it...

- The economic cost of hosting and keeping secure a competing network can easily be handled through the mining reward made available to blockchain miners.

  For example, on the bitcoin blockchain, miners compete for 12.5 bitcoins that become available every 10 minutes. Whoever solves a complex mathematical problem first gets the prize. At current prices, that's a $68,800 prize *every 10 minutes*.

  The investment the miners make in computer hardware going after the prize is what maintains the network. On the Ethereum network, miners receive five ether (or about $1,365) for solving its mathematical problems. But on the Ethereum network, blocks are produced every 15 seconds. So, the mining reward provides an economic incentive for miners to invest in the backbone of new networks.

- They're attracting new users by providing a platform that will pay them for their work.

So instead of receiving "likes," the people who create and curate the content all share in the profits of the network. When all participants have a stake in the success of the network, the profit motive is successfully harnessed to get all users working in the long-term best interest of the network.

One example of this model is a blockchain-powered social network called *Steemit*. Miners provide the computing power running the network. They compete for the mining reward for the successful completion of new blocks.

Steemit hit the 100,000 registered users mark in under five months. And it's holding its own against the current top social media sites. There are now more than 300,000 registered users creating, curating, and self-managing the Steemit network.

According to Alexa, Amazon's web analytics division, Steemit gets more daily pageviews per visitor than Facebook, Twitter, and Reddit.

Friends, that is remarkable because Steemit isn't even three years old yet. Think about that. In less than three years, the network has better page view metrics than every entrenched social media player in the space. That's amazing.

What Is Steemit?

Steemit is a social network in which users create and comment on each other's content. Steemit is made of subgroups that encompass literally thousands of topics.

Content creators write articles, how-tos, and opinion pieces on myriad topics. Users vote on the value of the content by "upvoting" good content and "downvoting" bad content.

This constant content curation leads to excellent articles becoming quickly recognized. That recognition pushes the content up the ranks on search engines like Google, which draws more users to the Steemit platform.

This creates a so-called "virtuous cycle" that seeks to make Steemit a globally trusted source of excellent content.

How Does It Work?

Content creators receive monetary rewards for their work when it is "liked." (Steemit uses the term upvoted.) These rewards vary. They depend on the amount of likes and the quality of the reputation of the people liking the content.

If someone has a high reputation score (all users start out with a reputation score of 25 and it tops out at 100), his or her upvote is much more valuable than an upvote from someone with a lower reputation score.

Will Steemit be the de facto leader in social media 10 years from now? Only time will tell. But one thing is for certain: The "old way" of social interaction online is phasing out, and making way for the new.

Making Online Gaming Trustworthy

Gambling is a global obsession. Worldwide, more than $500 billion per year is wagered in casinos. It's estimated that another $500 billion per year is spent on illegal sports betting *just in the United States*.

The market is vast, and yet online gaming is "just" $35 billion—or just about 7%—of the overall market.

There are lots of reasons online gaming has failed to gain the traction of traditional betting. One, of course, is legislation.

In the United States, online gambling rules aren't completely clear. It's legal in three states (Delaware, Nevada, and New Jersey), and online gaming legislation is close to being passed in California and Pennsylvania. And gambling laws vary across the globe. It's legal or unregulated in more than 60 countries.

Eventually, we think online gaming will be accepted... just like traditional gaming.

But for now, the biggest concern for online gamblers is trust.

Bettors are willing to risk their money with an online bookie... but they won't risk their money on an untrusted one. This is where the blockchain is primed to disrupt the gaming space. For the first time, gamblers will have access to provably fair gaming. That's because the blockchain can't be altered or manipulated.

There are many subsets in the gaming space. There are traditional casino games like roulette, craps, and poker. And person-to-person (P2P) gaming... like sports betting, and card games.

Instead of making a bet on just one of these applications, there is an App Coin that provides the development platform which will enable virtually any kind of gaming. We think taking the platform approach gives us a much better way to participate in the growth of blockchain gaming.

For example, a gaming platform called Peerplays allows players to bet directly against each other without the need of a middleman.

This is different from the current gaming model, which uses a "house" in the form of a casino or bookie. The system uses something called "smart contracts." These contracts contain the agreement of the bet.

The contracts handle collecting the money, safeguarding the money, and paying out the money. The contract is safeguarded from hacking or manipulation because it resides on the blockchain. Remember, it is very difficult and incredibly expensive to try to hack a blockchain.

Here's an example of how a smart contract might work:

Let's say you want to play a game of "who has the highest hand." You would go to a blockchain platform, select the game you want to play, and then enter in how much you want to bet.

From there, the smart contract will match you with another player. The smart contract collects the bets from both players and then begins the game. A provably fair random number generator will determine the "cards."

Once the cards are dealt, the players would have the choice to raise the bet. Assuming neither player chooses to raise the bet, each player's hand is revealed, and the winning player receives the pot.

With every winning hand, a small fee is "raked" off the top (around 2%). A tiny portion of the fee is reserved to cover mining rewards. Another small piece is carved off to go into a mega-jackpot. But the majority of the rake fees go to token holders.

Not only can you play real-money games… but you can also create real-money games.

The other thing that makes this different is that there is no "house" to bet against. When you go to a casino, you're betting against the "house." When you use a blockchain platform, you're given the opportunity to either be a player or to be "the house."

You can literally create your own online casino.

The biggest advantage of blockchain gaming over traditional gaming is something called provably fair gaming. Because this is all housed on a public blockchain, you have 100% confidence that no one is messing around with the odds.

You can't cheat on a blockchain gaming network. You're always going to get a fair game. No one in the online gambling world has been able to offer that... until now.

This blockchain model will turn the whole gaming world on its head.

Speeding Up International Trade

Matching buyers and sellers in financial markets is complex and very expensive. The largest expenses come from something called "trade settlement." This describes what happens after a buyer and seller agree to do a trade.

Hundreds of millions of trades involving hundreds of trillions of dollars have to be settled each year. The brokers for each party have to physically locate and deliver the shares that are being sold. The receiving brokers have to provide the funds and make sure the shares they're receiving are legitimate.

Making sure that what was agreed upon matches what is received is a problem that costs the banking and securities industry approximately $20 billion per year in trade settlement-related costs.

As you can imagine, having to double-check and match hundreds of millions of trades is a tedious job. All of this is still done by back-office staff. It's a wildly inefficient process, and that's why it takes up to four days to clear a trade.

The banks themselves very often abuse this inefficiency. For instance:

- In the late 1980s and early 1990s, Daiwa Securities Group, the massive Japanese brokerage firm, hid $1.1 billion in trading losses by manipulating the trade settlement system. Back then, it took 14 days to settle a trade. So, every 13 days, it would move the bad trades to a different account and start the whole settlement process all over again. It managed to get away with that for 11 years.

- State Street Bank recently paid $382 million to settle claims of fraudulent foreign currency exchange practices. Like Daiwa, State Street manipulated the trade settlement lag.

- Between 2013 and 2015, the world's biggest banks paid more than $60 billion in fines for manipulating the London Interbank Offered Rate (Libor). This is one of the most important interest rates in the world. Trillions in loans are pegged to Libor. Once again, banks manipulated the rate by taking advantage of the trade settlement delay.

Had trade settlement been on a blockchain, none of this fraud could have taken place. The immutability of the blockchain provides proof that all the participants on the network have the money they say they have... and the physical products they say they have (e.g. stocks, currencies, gold, etc.).

It also makes the kind of bid-rigging and loss-hiding of the big banks impossible. That's because trades would settle almost immediately. You wouldn't be able to avoid payment by continually bouncing the transaction between different accounts.

Whoever cracks instant trade settlement will gain a huge cost advantage over any other trade settlement platform. It could become the fastest and lowest-cost trade settlement platform in the world.

The company that ends up leading this market will have an insurmountable competitive edge against traditional exchanges. This application of the blockchain will kill traditional securities exchanges once and for all.

One blockchain example uses a trading platform that will let you buy and sell financial assets with zero commissions and near-instant (currently 15 minutes versus four days) trade settlement.

The platform has been used to test trade settlements on Swiss francs, euros, pounds, yens, and dollars.

Blockchains will make their money via the spread between the bid and offer price on trades. That will turn the entire industry upside down...

Improving Cyber Security

It's the biggest hijacking threat facing Americans today...

Every day, a small plane flies 18,000 feet above the sun-scorched Arizona desert on a secret mission to the U.S.-Mexico border.

And every day, the plane is under threat of being hijacked.

But this plane isn't taken over by some terrorist group. No passengers are taken hostage. Still, these "hijackings" cost American taxpayers hundreds of millions per year in wasted time and manpower.

You see, this plane is actually one of nine former military drones. They're part of a $300 million-per-year Department of Homeland Security (DHS) program to protect America's southern border.

It's a bold program... *and it's been an epic failure.*

Aside from costing $28,000 per hour to fly, the drones have one major problem: They're hackable.

Drug smugglers have figured out how to tamper with the drones' GPS. With the GPS compromised, they can essentially "hijack" the drones and divert them from their intended route.

The technique is called "spoofing."

Basically, hackers send signals that imitate the signal a drone was receiving. That effectively gives hackers control over the drone.

Once they "spoof" a drone, hackers can send it on a wild goose chase. They keep this up until the drone runs out of fuel.

When the drone is gone, the border is left wide open for smugglers to cross unimpeded.

As you can probably tell, this is a major problem for the DHS. But this kind of "spoofing" doesn't stop there.

Six billion everyday devices are already connected to the internet. And in three years, another 21 billion are expected to be connected.

This trend is called the Internet of Things (IoT).

Drones aren't the only devices that hackers can "spoof." They can "hijack" any device connected to the internet—smartphones, laptops, tablets, and even garage door openers, refrigerators, and microwaves.

In a meeting I attended in January 2017 with Under Secretary of Homeland Security Suzanne Spaulding, she said IoT devices represent the biggest security threat facing America.

I agree with her.

But the blockchain is creating a solution to this massive problem.

One blockchain network isolates the digital "fingerprints" of the devices it's protecting. It then encrypts the signature using an algorithm. The process is called "hashing."

A cryptographic hash is when you use a formula to transform a piece of data into a series of other numbers.

When you hash a specific piece of data (like a digital fingerprint from a drone), it will always give you the same string of characters.

But if you were to tamper with the device in any way, it would change the digital "fingerprint," which would then change the hash.

It's the equivalent of your identical twin trying to impersonate you. As soon as their fingerprints are taken, you would see that the prints don't match. One blockchain solution is like a fingerprint test for a machine.

The blockchain constantly checks the "fingerprint" identity of the machine.

As long as it remains the same, all is well. But if there is even the slightest change, the network immediately alerts the relevant authority that the device is being attacked.

To make sure that the "fingerprint" identity data itself can't be hacked, it's stored on the bitcoin blockchain.

Currently, no technology exists that can hack the bitcoin blockchain. It is the most secure computer network the world has ever known.

A New Way to Store Digital Data

Everyone, from soccer moms to global CEOs, relies on data storage. We use data storage to back up our kids' photos, our medical records, banking records, credit card information, and even our national secrets.

But there is a problem.

The current data-storage model is centralized. And that makes large databases juicy targets for hackers. When you store all your data on one centralized server, a hacker only has to break through a single line of defense to steal all of it.

Think of it like this...

Imagine you have a castle. In that castle, you have $1 million. Thieves only have to break through your walls to get your $1 million. It's difficult, but it's worth the gamble because the payoff is so large.

That's the problem with the centralized model of data storage. Each trove of data becomes a high-value target.

This dilemma is so obvious, you'd think everyone would take precautions... but they are not. Even our own government is still relying on centralized data storage.

Just look at the CIA.

The CIA maintains the world's most sophisticated computer hacking tools. These are the digital equivalents of a neutron bomb. And the CIA keeps this treasure trove of digital weaponry on a *central* server.

In early March 2017, that server was hacked, and our greatest digital weapons are now in the hands of our enemies.

It's not just the CIA. From November to December 2013, 70 million Target accounts were hacked. Yahoo has been a victim as well. Separate attacks in 2013 and 2014 affected over 1.5 billion accounts.

According to ZDNet, there were 3,000 reported breaches exposing over 2.2 billion records in 2016. Notable victims include LinkedIn, SWIFT (the global banking transfer system), and the National Security Agency (NSA).

The NSA breach is the most alarming. Hackers stole the NSA's own hacking tools and then auctioned them off.

The list goes on and on. It's estimated that data breaches cost $600 billion per year. Juniper Research expects this to increase to $2.1 trillion by 2019.

But there is a solution to this vulnerability.

Creating 1 Million "Mini" Castles

The solution is called decentralized storage via the blockchain. Let's go back to our castle example.

Imagine that instead of having one castle with $1 million in it, we had 1 million castles that each had a single dollar. For $1, what are the odds anyone would even attack your castle?

Very low, right?

Breaking into a castle to steal $1 is just not worth it. And the costs to breaking into 1 million castles to steal the entire $1 million would be astronomical.

That's the power of a decentralized model.

You don't keep the data in one place. You split it up, encrypt it, and disperse it. That makes any attack against your data costly.

Decentralized storage is the future of data storage. Everything from your photos to your most sensitive data will be stored this way. Large-scale data hacks will become a thing of the past.

But how practical is it to build 1 million castles just to protect $1 in value? Not very, right?

That's the reason data-storage giants like Amazon, Apple, and Google don't use decentralized storage—it's too expensive. The cost of building just one "data castle" is $600 million.

But what if you could "borrow" 1 million castles and keep $1 in each of them?

Suddenly, the economics start making sense.

That's where the sharing economy comes into play.

One blockchain company has developed a tool using the Blockchain that lets you lease space on other people's hard drives.

It might sound confusing, but it's actually simple. It takes your data, splits it up, encrypts it, and then stores it on hundreds of computers. No one can read what's been stored. Only you—the user—can retrieve and restore the data.

The company doesn't own any of the computers in its network. It just provides the platform to rent out computing space.

This new model of decentralized storage will disrupt an industry that's been dominated by centralized databases owned by Amazon and Dropbox.

Chapter 10:
Blockchain Is the Future

Think about how big this all is.

Real estate transactions have been done basically the same way since the Middle Ages. So has global trade. Each has been a cumbersome, paperwork-heavy process that takes months.

In a few years, the blockchain will allow you to qualify for a loan, conduct a title search, and close on a house in a single day. It's not that far off.

In a few years, every single business on the planet will conduct transactions on the blockchain.

And each business will have a cross-border payroll system on the blockchain... national borders will become irrelevant. People from all over the world will be able to seamlessly work together in the same organization, regardless of location.

In a few years, all stocks and bonds will be traded on the blockchain. Wall Street and crony regulators will only exist as an exhibit in the Smithsonian Museum.

In a few years, global ID systems will be on the blockchain. Instead of a national ID card, like a passport, you will be able to create your own blockchain-based ID.

This ID will be transnational—it won't tie you to a particular country. Instead, your blockchain ID will tie into your private keys that control your cryptocurrencies.

And unlike your passport, your private key is based on an alphanumeric code. You won't have to use your picture, name, or address for a blockchain ID.

In fact, independent blockchain ID systems already exist. Onename. com maintains a blockchain ID system. So does Bitnation.co.

You can think of these systems as credit reports for the blockchain. Except they will not be managed by credit reporting companies… they will be automated by smart contracts.

That is how you will be able to close on a house in a single day. Smart contracts will instantly verify your qualifying information because it will already be on the blockchain.

To initiate a smart contract with someone on the blockchain, you don't need to know their name, address, nationality, or anything else about them. All you need to know is that their blockchain ID verifies they have the assets necessary to complete any deal you make with them.

Like past technologies, blockchain IDs will not catch on right away. But these systems will become useful as people conduct more and more business on the blockchain.

Here are two reasons blockchain ID systems will be prevalent in a few years.

First, they are based on the premise of voluntary interaction. Unlike the government's ID system, nobody will force blockchain IDs on you. Remember, these IDs aren't tied to your picture, name, or address… And they don't use biometric data like fingerprints or DNA. They're tied to your crypto private keys.

You will still be free to conduct transactions anonymously if you choose to. But certain businesses and trade groups will require you to have a blockchain ID before they will deal with you.

For example, a company specializing in mortgage lending on the blockchain may require you to have an established blockchain ID before they will lend money to you. That means you will need to build up your blockchain reputation by participating in the crypto economy before taking out the mortgage—just like you must build up your credit history in the legacy system today.

The second thing you need to know is that blockchain IDs will be reputation-based. Reputation trumps credentials in the Information Age.

Instead of tying you to the actions of your national government, like your passport does, your blockchain ID will hold you accountable for your own actions. If you are a decent person, your blockchain ID will be welcomed anywhere in the world. You will be free to travel and trade across borders.

But if you are a bad actor—if you commit violence, theft, or fraud—your actions will be recorded on the blockchain. And your blockchain ID will tell the world to be careful around you. You will not be welcomed to travel or trade in certain places. Others will deal with you very cautiously... if at all.

If that sounds too Orwellian, remember that these systems will not be managed by governments or central parties... they will be automated by smart contracts. And these contracts will be created by free associations of people.

This is going to radically change how our "law enforcement" system operates once blockchain-based transactions become the norm.

Instead of cops, prisons, and punishment, criminals will be shunned by free communities. They will be locked out of trade and travel associations. They will not be welcomed in many places until they have proven themselves to be "reformed" by engaging in honest transactions with others.

The blockchain ID reputation system will radically reduce crime rates because crime will no longer pay. Crime will make you an outcast... forever. It will be very hard for criminals to maintain a decent standard of living.

As a result, the blockchain will radically change the form and function of the nation-state.

If you didn't know, the nation-states of today are relatively new. They didn't exist for most of our history.

Upon its founding 1776, the United States was actually the "united States." It was not one giant country. It was thirteen small countries, or "states."

The same was true for most of Europe prior to the 19th century. Instead of giant nation-states, Europe consisted of much smaller entities—each with its own culture and traditions.

I don't think the nation-states we know today will go away entirely... but they will become much less important.

In a few years, there will be crypto-states on the blockchain. Crypto-states will be like "voluntary" governments. They will each have their own systems, rules, and functions... but no one will be forced to participate or pay taxes. You will be free to choose your own associations according to your own principles and values.

By the way, this is not a fantasy. The first crypto-state is already here. It is called BitNation.

BitNation offers a blockchain ID, blockchain notary services, emergency response services, ambassador support, citizen security services, an education network, and even a space agency.

What's more, BitNation provides the infrastructure for anyone to create their own crypto-state using their existing framework. Just like there are now 1,000 App Coins in existence, one day there will be 1,000 crypto-states.

Each crypto-state will be different from the next. Some of them will be based on values that you don't share. Some will strike you as immoral.

But that's no different than our circumstances with nation-states today. The difference is, nothing will be forced upon you. You will be free to deal only with the people you want to deal with.

These crypto-states will be looked down upon at first. Nation-states will try to destroy them.

But they will keep popping up because they will be 100% virtual. All their administrative functions will be handled autonomously on the blockchain. These crypto-states will basically be "ideas" encoded into the blockchain. You can't kill an idea.

Putting it all together, blockchain technology is going to lead to a new *Renaissance* for human civilization. We will talk about that at the end of the book.

But first, we need to go over everything you need to know to buy, trade, and store cryptocurrencies so you can participate in the blockchain revolution.

Chapter 11:
The Cryptocurrency Quick-Start Guide

I know I have thrown a lot at you so far. If you are new to all of this, don't worry; we'll show you everything you need to get started with cryptocurrencies.

The easiest way to understand how cryptocurrencies work is to compare them to traditional stock trading.

The picture below shows the traditional stock trading ecosystem. As you can see, you take funds from your bank account and send it to your brokerage account. Then, your broker connects you to the exchanges where you can buy stocks, bonds, options, etc. When you sell, the process reverses. Money from a stock you sell goes back to your brokerage account and then to your bank account if you choose.

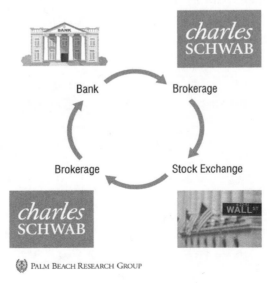

The traditional stock trading ecosystem is well-developed. That's why you can get away with using just one service, like Charles Schwab in the picture above.

The cryptocurrency ecosystem is still in its infancy. It's not as built out as the traditional stock trading ecosystem. Therefore, we may need to use two or more services to accomplish our goals.

Cryptocurrency Lesson No. 1

Here's the first thing you need to know about cryptocurrencies: The entire space is still very young and being developed.

It is not yet at the same point the stock ecosystem is, where you can get everything done through one service.

That makes it a bit more difficult to get into the cryptocurrency space. But that difficulty is also our opportunity—an opportunity to get in before everyone else.

The Cryptocurrency Ecosystem

Below is a picture of the cryptocurrency ecosystem. It's similar to the traditional system. However, the services are a bit different. Don't worry if you are not familiar with these services. We'll review each later in this chapter.

With the cryptocurrency ecosystem, it all starts with converting your local currency to bitcoin. Then, you use cryptocurrency wallets to store your cryptocurrencies.

And you use cryptocurrency exchanges to buy and sell cryptocurrencies. In a minute, we'll go over how it all works together in more detail.

Cryptocurrency Lesson No. 2

While the traditional stock system operates through brokerages such as Charles Schwab, in the cryptocurrency system, we use cryptocurrency wallets and cryptocurrency exchanges.

What exactly is a cryptocurrency wallet? A cryptocurrency wallet is a secure digital wallet to store, send, and receive a digital currency like bitcoin.

And what is a cryptocurrency exchange? It's an online platform where you can buy, sell, or exchange cryptocurrencies for other digital currencies.

What's important to understand is that cryptocurrencies cannot be bought through traditional brokerage accounts. For example, if you go to your Schwab or Fidelity account and try to buy BTC (the symbol for bitcoin), you'll end up with Bangpakong Terminal PCL, not bitcoin.

You cannot buy cryptocurrencies on a traditional stock exchange.

What Else Do I Need to Know?

We typically recommend trading with a buy-up-to price and stop loss. So, what are those?

A buy-up-to price is the maximum price you want to pay for a cryptocurrency or stock. It's designed so that you never overpay for a cryptocurrency or stock.

We tend to think of buy-up-to prices in terms of U.S. dollars. However, cryptocurrencies are generally priced in bitcoin. So how do you get from one price to the other?

Simply use the CoinDesk bitcoin calculator. You type in the bitcoin price, and it will give you the U.S. dollar price.

A stop loss is a capital preservation strategy designed to limit your losses.

Due to the volatility of cryptocurrencies (meaning they have big price swings), it is difficult to set a prudent stop loss. So, we also highly recommend that you use prudent position sizes. **That means not investing more than you are comfortable losing**.

Let's go over how these risk management strategies work.

Suppose you are looking at a new cryptocurrency—ABC coin for example. ABC coin is currently trading at $1 per coin, and you think it could easily double after a software update is released next month.

A buy-up-to price of $1.50 would be reasonable in this example. This allows you to scale into ABC coin—making several small purchases over the next several weeks—as long as the price does not move higher than $1.50 per coin.

But ABC coin is a speculative cryptocurrency, so you don't want to put too much money into it. This is where position-sizing comes into play. We typically recommend that you put no more than 1-2% of your money into any speculative asset—including small cryptocurrencies.

For ABC coin, let's use a 1% position size. So, if your total portfolio is $100,000, you should only invest $1,000 in ABC coin.

Stop losses are the final piece of our risk management puzzle. A stop loss is a predetermined price at which you will sell your cryptocurrency no matter what.

For ABC coin, let's use a stop loss of $0.50. So, if ABC coin ever falls to $0.50 in price, we will sell our entire position to preserve our capital.

Here's how powerful these simple risk management strategies are when used together.

Suppose we buy ABC coin at $1.00 with a 1% position size—that's a $1,000 investment in this example. And suppose we learn that ABC coin's software upgrade has been delayed... and the cryptocurrency plummets in value, hitting our stop loss. We sell our entire position as soon as it falls to $0.50—booking a $500 loss.

Our loss on ABC coin was 50%... but the total loss to our portfolio was only .005% ($500/$100,000).

We won't lose any sleep over a .005% loss. That is why these risk management strategies are crucial in the cryptocurrency space.

Okay, now that we've gone over the basics, you're ready to start buying cryptocurrencies.

Cryptocurrency Lesson No. 3

Remember this from above: Buying cryptocurrencies starts with converting your local currency to bitcoin.

And this is where the process can get confusing for those new to cryptocurrencies.

Not all cryptocurrency services support conversion from your local currency to bitcoin.

In other words, with some cryptocurrency wallets, you can exchange your local currency for bitcoin. But with others, you cannot. Same for the exchanges. Some offer local currency conversion, while others don't.

What's the Right Service for You?

We would love to give you a precise answer.

But there is no right answer. The truth is: It depends. The right services to use depend on you and your needs.

This guide will cover all the services we use and recommend so you can make an informed decision on what works best for you.

Your First Step With Cryptocurrencies – Buying Bitcoin

The first step is to convert your local currency to bitcoin. Remember from Cryptocurrency Lesson No. 3 that not all services offer this feature. Below is a list of services that offer conversion of your local currency to bitcoin.

Services for Converting U.S. Dollars to Bitcoin				
Name	**Type**	**App or PC**	**What can you buy?**	**Is it good for storage?**
Gemini	Exchange	PC	Bitcoin & ether	No
Coinbase	Wallet	Both	Bitcoin & ether	No
Abra	Wallet	App	Bitcoin	Yes
Airbitz	Wallet	App	Bitcoin	Yes

As you can see from the list, at the time of this writing, we have four choices for converting U.S. dollars to bitcoin.

Let's go over the differences between the services. Coinbase, Abra, and Airbitz are all wallets, while Gemini is an exchange.

Coinbase is the only one available for both PC and smartphones as an app. Abra and Airbitz are available as smartphone apps only. Gemini is available only on PC.

For storage, we recommend storing bitcoin where you have control of the private key. Both Abra and Airbitz check this box. (A private key is the code you use to access your bitcoin wallet.)

Coinbase does not give you control of your private key. It does this to make its product easier to use. However, without the private key, you lack complete control. Therefore, we recommended that if you buy bitcoin on Coinbase, you store any long-term holdings in a wallet where you control the private key. (We'll provide a list of alternative wallets in a moment.)

In general, we recommend that you do not use any of the exchanges for storage. These are centralized services where you do not control the private keys. Therefore, there's an element of risk to holding coins on an exchange.

For example, if you use the Gemini exchange to buy bitcoin, then we would recommend moving any long-term holdings into an alternative wallet.

Storing Bitcoin and Other Cryptocurrencies

After buying your first bitcoin, you're going to need a place to store it.

That's where cryptocurrency wallets come in.

As we learned from the section above, Abra, Airbitz, and Coinbase are all bitcoin wallets. But we only recommend storing your bitcoin and other cryptocurrencies in Abra and Airbitz. That's because you don't have complete control of your private key with Coinbase. However, there are additional wallets you can use. Check out the list:

Bitcoin Wallets		
Name	**USD**	**Notes**
Abra	Yes	Only available as an app
Airbitz	Yes	Only available as an app
Jaxx	No	PC, app, Chrome extension
Blockchain.info	No	PC and app
Paper wallets	No	Video to come
Hardwire wallets	No	Video to come

In addition to Abra and Airbitz, we also have the Jaxx wallet and the Blockchain.info wallet.

Unlike Abra and Airbitz, these wallets do not allow users to convert U.S. dollars to bitcoin. They are good, however, for storing bitcoin.

Both Jaxx and Blockchain.info have the added advantage of being available both on your PC and smartphone. And Jaxx has the additional feature of supporting multiple cryptocurrencies for storage.

Paper wallets and hardwire wallets are two additional ways to store your bitcoin with additional layers of safety.

Cryptocurrency Exchanges

Once you are able to buy bitcoin and store it safely, the next step is to sign up to cryptocurrency exchanges so you can buy other cryptocurrencies.

The next table shows the major exchanges we recommend:

Services for Buying Cryptocurrencies for Bitcoin		
Name	**USD**	**What can you purchase?**
Bittrex	No	Over 190 cyrptocurrencies
Gemini	Yes	Bitcoin and ether
Kraken	Yes	Bitcoin, ether, + 40 others
Coinbase	Yes	Bitcoin, ether, and Litecoin

At the time of publication, one of the most popular cryptocurrency exchanges in the United States is Bittrex. It offers over 190 cryptocurrencies to buy.

Please note that Bittrex does not offer the option to directly deposit your local currency to the exchange. To use these exchanges, you'll need to buy bitcoin first then transfer your bitcoin to the exchange.

The next exchange is Gemini. While the Gemini exchange does offer currency conversion, only two cryptocurrencies are available to buy: bitcoin and ether. If you are looking to buy additional cryptocurrencies, you'll need to transfer your bitcoin from the Gemini exchange to another exchange.

Another exchange is Coinbase. While Coinbase does offer currency conversion, only three cryptocurrencies are available to buy: bitcoin, ether, and Litecoin. If you are looking to buy additional cryptocurrencies, you'll need to transfer your bitcoin from Coinbase to another exchange such as Bittrex.

Finally, there is the Kraken exchange. It does offer local currency conversion, but it must be done through a wire, so you are subjected to wire fees.

Kraken offers dozens of cryptocurrencies you can buy.

Crypto Guide Wrap-Up

This is a brief overview of the services you need to get started.

To start using cryptocurrencies today, begin by buying bitcoin with your local currency. Review the five services listed above and choose the right one for you. You may even find it's in your best interest to use multiple services.

The next step is to download a wallet for bitcoin storage. Again, the best one depends on your circumstances. For example, if you don't own a smartphone, you would want to avoid using Abra or Airbitz.

Finally, sign up to one of the exchanges so you can convert bitcoin into other cryptocurrencies.

Pro Tips

Do I have to buy a whole bitcoin?

No, a bitcoin is divisible to the eighth decimal point. That means the smallest unit of bitcoin, called a Satoshi, is 0.00000001 bitcoin.

You can buy any dollar amount of bitcoin you want.

I'm new to cryptocurrencies and still gaining comfort with the services. What can I do so that I don't lose my money?

First, take some time to learn about the services before you use them.

Second, when you start using a service, test it out with small transactions. That way, if you don't like the service or run into problems, you have taken very little risk.

And third, most problems arise from transferring coins from one service to another. Before you hit send, make sure you are sending to the right wallet. For example, you do not want to send bitcoin to an ether wallet. Also, double-check the address before sending. A quick way is to check the first four and last four characters of the address. As long as they match up, you're good to go.

I sent bitcoin from Coinbase to Bittrex, but it's not showing up. What do I do?

This problem is not specific to Coinbase and Bittrex. It can happen with any service.

First, check the address. If you entered the wrong address, you would need to contact the receiver. In this case, it's Bittrex. It may be able to recover the funds.

Second, check your email. You may need to confirm the transaction by clicking on a link sent to you via email.

Third, it's possible your transaction just hasn't been confirmed yet. Remember: On the bitcoin blockchain, a block is generated roughly every 10 minutes.

I signed up to Abra, but the limit is too low. What can I do?

There are a few actions you can take to increase your limits. The first is to sign up with multiple services. Then, your combined limit will increase with each service added.

The next action you can take is providing additional identity verification. Each service has a section where you can provide additional information.

Finally, you can get your limits increased by consistently making small purchases. For example, you could purchase $25 worth of bitcoin every two weeks. This will help to develop the relationship and will result in periodic limit increases.

The wallet for my cryptocurrency at Bittrex or Gemini is temporarily disabled. What does this mean?

It means that Bittrex or Gemini is performing regularly scheduled maintenance on the wallet.

This is normal. Wallet functionality is generally back up and running within 24 hours.

We will talk about the different wallets in a little more detail in the next chapter.

Chapter 12:
How to Buy and Store Cryptocurrencies

Now that you've learned how powerful and profitable cryptocurrencies will be, it's time to learn how to buy them and keep them safe. This chapter will show you:

- How to set up an Abra account. Abra allows you to buy bitcoins.

- How to set up an account using Bittrex. Bittrex is a cryptocurrency-trading exchange. We'll show you how to send bitcoins to Bittrex, so you can exchange it for other cryptocurrencies including ether.

- How to set up an ether wallet. You'll need an ether wallet to store your ether.

Setting Up an Abra Wallet

Abra is a digital wallet that works with <u>over 50 currencies</u>, including bitcoin. Abra allows you to link your bank account and buy bitcoins with the click of a button.

This guide will show you how to download Abra onto your smartphone. In our example, we downloaded Abra onto an iPhone.

Step 1—Search for the Abra app

- Type in "Abra" on your App Store or Google Play Store search bar.

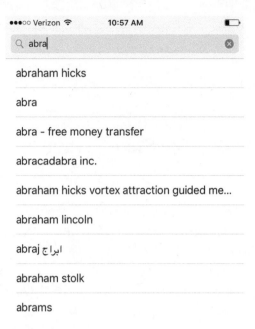

abraham hicks

abra

abra - free money transfer

abracadabra inc.

abraham hicks vortex attraction guided me...

abraham lincoln

abraj ابراج

abraham stolk

abrams

Step 2—Download Abra

- Click the "Get" or "Download" button.

Once downloaded, it will appear on your phone's home screen.

Step 3—Signing Up

- Open the app. This is what the front page should look like:

- Click "SIGN UP." It will take you to this page and ask you to enter your cellphone number:

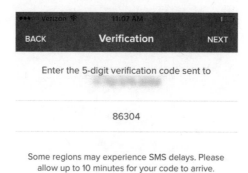

- Once you enter your number, Abra will text you a verification code. Open the text to access it.

- Enter the code into the Abra app.

- Click next. Then, create your profile by entering your name and email address.

- Click next to create a pin to secure your Abra wallet. (Make sure it's a pin number you can remember. You'll need to enter it every time you access the app.)

Step 4—Connecting your bank account

- You are now ready to use Abra. This is what your front page should look like now:

- To link your bank account, click "Add Money." On the next page, click "Use Bank Account."

- Then click the "Add Bank Account" button.

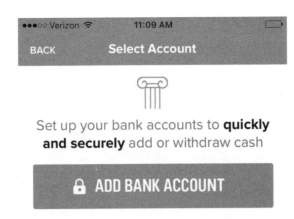

- Abra supports most major banks. Scroll through and select your bank.

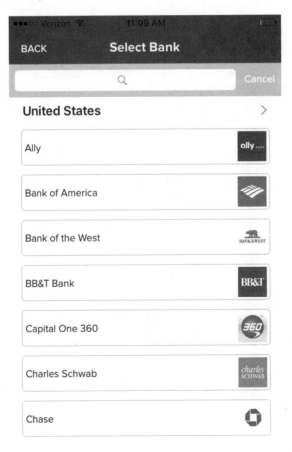

Step 5—Verify your identity

- Once you have selected your bank, you will be prompted to verify your identity. Fill in the information on the page.

```
┌─────────────────────────────────────┐
│  BACK        Verify Your Identity   │
├─────────────────────────────────────┤
│  Enter the following information to  │
│  verify your identity               │
│  ─────────────────────────────────  │
│  FIRST NAME:                        │
│  ─────────────────────────────────  │
│  LAST NAME:                         │
│  ─────────────────────────────────  │
│  EMAIL:                             │
│  ─────────────────────────────────  │
│  DATE OF BIRTH:  MM/DD/YYY          │
│  ─────────────────────────────────  │
│    STREET                           │
│  ADDRESS:                           │
│  ─────────────────────────────────  │
│  ZIP CODE:                          │
│  ─────────────────────────────────  │
│  By creating this account you agree │
│  to our financial software partner  │
│  SynapsePays Terms of Service &     │
│  Privacy Policy                     │
│  (https://synapsepay.com/legal).    │
│  ─────────────────────────────────  │
│  ┌───────────────────────────────┐  │
│  │            NEXT               │  │
│  └───────────────────────────────┘  │
└─────────────────────────────────────┘
```

- You will then be asked to log into your bank account. This is the username and password you use to log into your online or mobile bank account.

- Abra uses a secure connection to do this and doesn't store any of your credentials.

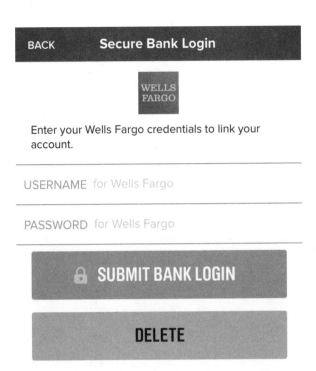

- Your bank will send you an email with a verification code. Retrieve the code from your email and enter it where prompted. When you're done, click "Verify."

Step 6—Change currency to bitcoin

- Click on the menu button at the top left of the app. This will take you to Settings. Scroll down and click on "Wallet Currency."

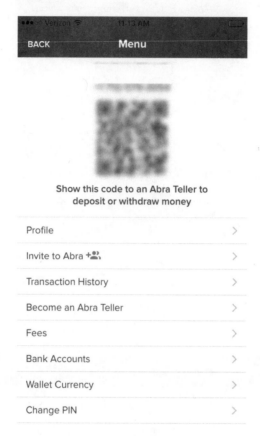

- Change the currency by clicking on "US Dollar $USD."

- Abra will provide a list of currencies it supports. Click on "Bitcoin BTC" to change currency to bitcoin.

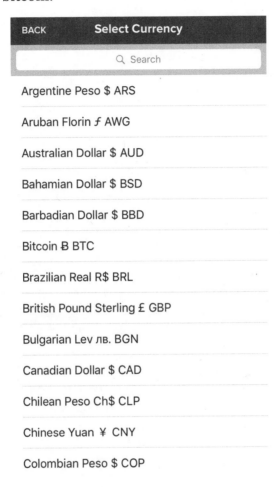

Step 7—Create a backup wallet

- Click the menu button at the top left of the app. Select "Backup."

Show this code to an Abra Teller to
deposit or withdraw money

Profile	>
Invite to Abra +🧑	>
Transaction History	>
Become an Abra Teller	>
Fees	>
Bank Accounts	>
Wallet Currency	>
Change PIN	>
Backup	>

- The backup is a 12-word phrase. Be sure you write it down and store it someplace safe. You can use the backup phrase to restore your wallet if anything happens to your phone.

Step 8—Buying Bitcoin

- On the front page of the app, click "Add Money." When prompted on how you want to buy bitcoin, click "Use Bank Account."

MY BALANCE

$0.00
US Dollar

+ ADD MONEY

SEND

REQUEST PAYMENT

WITHDRAW

- Then click on the bank account you connected earlier.

- Abra will prompt you to enter the amount. Enter how much bitcoin you want to buy in USD.

- Confirm your transaction and press "OK"

Congratulations! You now own bitcoin.

How to Convert Bitcoin Into Ether and Other Cryptocurrencies

To convert bitcoin into ether, you will need to use a cryptocurrency exchange. In the previous chapter, we introduced you to some of the largest ones out there. We are going to cover Bittrex in this chapter.

Bittrex is a U.S.-based exchange offering maximum security and advanced trading features. It's the No. 1 U.S.-based exchange by volume.

Here's how to set up a Bittrex account.

Step 1—Create an account

- Go to the Bittrex home page

- Click the "Get Started Now" button on the home page.

- Fill in the requested information...

Step 2—Verify your email address

- After creating your account, Bittrex will send you an email.

- Open the email and click the link to verify your email address.

Step 3—Verify your account

- At the top right corner of the website, click "Settings." Select "Basic Verification" on the left.

- Fill out all the information to verify your identity, including your name, birthday, and address. Passport number is optional.

- Verify your cellphone by selecting "Phone Verification" on the left and inputting your number.

- Bittrex will send you an SMS with a security code. Enter that in the box when it appears.

Step 4—Set up two-factor authentication (recommended)

- Follow the instructions to download Google Authenticator and enable two-factor authentication.

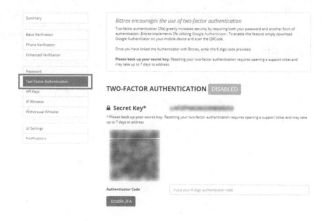

Buying Ether

Let's focus on buying ether in Bittrex for this example.

With Bittrex, the only way to acquire ether, or other cryptocurrencies for that matter, is with bitcoin. Here's how to transfer bitcoin to your Bittrex account from your Abra account.

Step 1

- Click on the "Wallets" tab (in red).

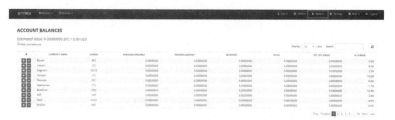

- The page will list all the cryptocurrencies you can deposit and withdraw.

Step 2

- The first cryptocurrency you will see listed is bitcoin. If you don't see it, type "BTC" into the search box and it will pop up.

- Click on the plus symbol to the left of the listing:

Step 3

- A box will pop up to generate an address you can use to send your bitcoin from a wallet or exchange to Bittrex.

- Click "New Address."

- Bittrex will generate an address. Copy the address.

- It is important to read the warning. Sending any cryptocurrency besides bitcoin to this address will result in the loss of tokens.

Step 4

- Log into your Abra account.

Step 5

- Click "Use Bitcoin."

Step 6

- In the "To" box, paste the address you generated from Bittrex. Or scan the QR code using the camera on your smartphone.

- Enter the amount of bitcoin you want to send. Click "Next" on the top right corner.

Step 7

- Review the information. Click "Confirm Withdrawal."

Step 8

- Go back to Bittrex.

- Click on the "Wallets" tab.

- In a few minutes, you should see your pending deposit in this section:

- The transaction needs to be confirmed before you can start using your bitcoins on the exchange.

Bitcoin transactions generally take 10 minutes to confirm, so don't panic if you don't immediately see your bitcoin in Bittrex.

Step 9

- To convert your bitcoin to ether, click on the "Bitcoin Markets" tab.

- Type in ETH, and select the entry when it pops up.

Step 10

- This will take you to the ether information page:

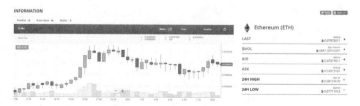

- This page will show a history of what prices ether traded at and is currently trading at on Bittrex.

Step 11

- On the exchange page, below the price chart, you will find the windows to buy and sell ether (see picture below).

Step 12

- To buy ether, go to the "Buy Ethereum" box and enter the total amount of bitcoin you would like to convert.

- The corresponding amount of ETH will automatically populate.

Step 13

- Click "Buy."

- You must wait a few minutes for the order to complete.

Step 14

- To see your order, go to the "Orders" tab at the top right of the page. This will show all open and completed orders.

Congratulations! You now own ether, the cryptocurrency of Ethereum. And you can use the above process to transfer bitcoin to other cryptocurrencies as well.

How to Store Your Cryptocurrencies

To store your cryptos, you have several options.

Option 1:

You can simply keep your coins on the Bittrex exchange. But we don't advise this.

The advantage of this option is you'll have quick and easy access to your cryptos if you want to trade them. The downside is if Bittrex is hacked, you could lose your cryptos.

Bittrex constantly upgrades and tests its systems to ensure it is exceeding industry best standards. To protect users, Bittrex requires two-factor authentication for withdrawals. Bittrex.com is also protected by Secure Sockets Layer (SSL), a protocol for transmitting private documents via the internet.

Option 2:

Store your bitcoins in your bitcoin wallet and your ether in your ether wallet. This makes sense if you hold any significant amount of funds in either.

To transfer ether to your wallet, go back to the "Wallets" tab in Bittrex. Type "ETH" into the search bar. Then click the minus button in the Ethereum row, to the left of the listing.

Fill in your ether wallet address and the amount you want to send, then click "Withdrawal." Double-check your ether wallet to confirm the transaction completed.

Practice sending small amounts back and forth from Abra and Bittrex, along with your wallets. To take extra care, you can make sure you keep some cryptos in each exchange to ensure you don't hold everything in one place.

How to Set Up MyEtherWallet

MyEtherWallet is a tool for generating ether wallets and sending transactions.

Step 1

- Go to the MyEtherWallet website: https://www.myetherwallet.com/

Step 2

- Make sure the "Generate Wallet" tab on the far left is selected.

- Enter a strong password, then select "Generate Wallet."

- Save the password somewhere safe.

Step 3

- After you generate your wallet, MyEtherWallet will create a public and private key for you. See the picture below.

- The public key is the same as your address (No. 1 in the photo). You will receive a QR code (No. 3) and an alpha-numeric address (No. 1). You do not need to use both. Think of your address (or public key) as "incoming." This is the address you will use to receive ether.

- The private key is Nos. 2 and 4 in the photo. Again, you're provided with a QR code and an alpha-numeric address. Think of your private key as "outgoing." This is the address you will use to send ether. The private key is the one you need to store securely.

- Before you make another move: Back up your private key externally and verify that you can access the wallet. Meaning: Save it somewhere secure, like on a hard drive you keep stored at home or in a lockbox. And practice accessing it. Do this before you buy any ether. MyEtherWallet cannot recover your wallet, so it's imperative that you save your private key and password.

- Do not show anyone your private key. You need it to access your wallet and to move, spend, or send ether.

Step 4

- Store your address, private key, and PDF of your paper wallet in a folder on your computer.

Step 5

- Put your folder on a USB drive. For extra security, encrypt the USB drive.

Step 6

- Before you send any ether to your new wallet, ensure you have access to it.

- Do not copy and paste from the "Generate Wallet" tab. Instead, copy and paste from the text document or the document where you have stored your wallet information.

Step 7—Sending ether

- Click the "Send Transaction" tab.

- You will see the following:

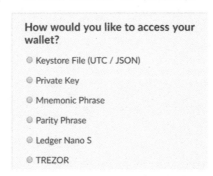

- Click the "Private Key" button. Copy and paste your private key into the box provided.

- You can now send ETH to that address and be certain you can access it.

Chapter 13:
Guide to Cryptocurrency Wallets

After you purchase your cryptocurrencies, it's crucial you store them somewhere safe. You'll hear stories of hacks and people's bitcoin or other cryptocurrency being wiped out. We want to make sure that doesn't happen to you.

That's why we recommend you store your cryptocurrency in a wallet whenever possible and take precautions to guard your private keys.

We've compared some of our favorite cryptocurrency wallets. Look at the table below to see which one best fits your needs. Then, use our guides to set up your cryptocurrency wallet.

We are going to go over how to set up a wallet with Jaxx and Blockchain.info in this chapter.

Compare Wallets	Abra	Jaxx	Blockchain.info
Ease of Use	Easy	Average	Easy
Mobile	Yes	Yes	Yes
Web Interface	No	Yes	Yes
Desktop Client	No	Yes	No
Cryptocurrencies Supported	BTC	BTC, ETH, ETC, DASH, DAO, LTC, REP, ZEC	BTC
Two-Factor Authentication	No	No	Yes
Allows Fiat Conversion	Yes	No	No

Anonymity	Low	High	Average
Security	Average	High	Average
Cost	Free *	Network fees ^	Free ~

* The use of Abra's wallet service are free. Fiat conversion is currently available in the United States and the Philippines.

^ Fees applied to transactions support the network that runs the coin/token. The fees for bitcoin are dynamic. They go up and down based on the state of the network.

~ The blockchain.info wallet service is free of charge. However, an additional network fee maybe required for some smaller transactions, which go to the bitcoin miners.

(Prices and information as of April 2017)

Setting up a Jaxx Wallet

Jaxx supports several cryptocurrencies, including bitcoin, ether, and others. Its goal is to support all cryptocurrencies.

With Jaxx, you can also easily restore your account using your backup passphrase in case something happens to your computer or phone.

Step 1—Go to the Jaxx website at <ins>https://jaxx.io/support.html</ins>

Step 2—Install Jaxx

- There are many ways to download the Jaxx wallet. Choose whichever is most convenient for you.
- In this example, we'll be downloading a Google Chrome extension for Jaxx.

Step 3—Create a new wallet

- Once you add the extension, click on the icon on the top right-hand corner of your browser.

- Click "Create New Wallet."

Step 4—Save your backup phrase

- Click the options menu.

- Click "Tools."

- Click the first option, "Display Backup Phrase."

- Clicking "Proceed to Backup" will show your backup phrase. Write it down and save it somewhere secure. Remember, if something happens to your computer, your backup phrase will restore your wallet.

- After that, Jaxx will ask you to confirm your backup phrase. This is where you will fill in the words you wrote down.

Step 5—Find different cryptocurrencies

- You can bring up information on different coins by scrolling through the tabs at the top. Each coin has a unique address.

Step 6—Sending bitcoin

- Go to the bitcoin tab and click the "Send" tab at the top.

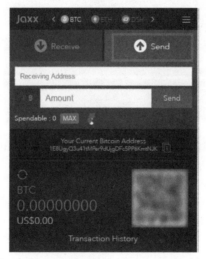

- Copy the address listed.

- Go to Coinbase or another wallet you are using and paste that address.

- It will send bitcoin from Jaxx to that account.

Step 7—Receiving bitcoins

- Click the "Receive" button. Fill in the amount you want to receive in your Jaxx wallet, and it will generate a bitcoin address for you.

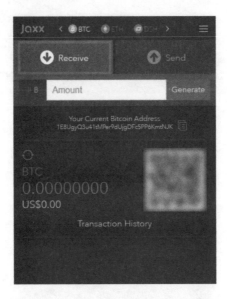

Setting up a Blockchain.info Wallet

The Blockchain.info wallet is the most-used wallet in the world. It's web-based and easy to use.

Step 1—Go to the Blockchain.info website

- Go to the Blockchain.info website at: https://blockchain.info/wallet/#/

Step 2—Create a wallet

- Click on the "Get Started Now" button.

- Fill in your information and press "Continue."

Blockchain.info will send you an email with your identifier.

Step 3—Access your wallet

- The tabs on the left help you manage your Blockchain. info wallet.

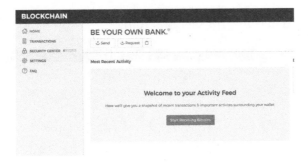

Step 4—Secure your wallet

- Click "Security Center" tab.

- Complete all the security levels by verifying your email address, saving your backup security phrase, creating a password hint, and linking your cellphone number.

Step 5—Enable two-step authentication

- Blockchain.info uses Google Authenticator. You can download the app on your smart phone or access it at: https://play.google.com/store/apps/details?id=com. google.android.apps.authenticator2&hl=en

Step 6—Sending bitcoin

- Go to the "Transactions" tab.

- Click the "Send" button and follow the instructions.

Step 7: Receiving bitcoin

- Click the "Request" button in the "Transactions" tab.

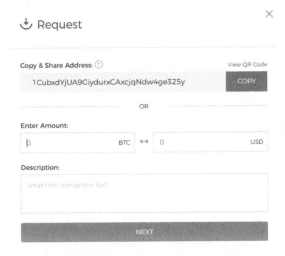

- Copy the address and share it with the person you will be receiving bitcoins from.

- You can also paste this address into Coinbase or one of your other wallets to transfer your own bitcoins from one wallet to another.

Chapter 14:
The International Guide to Buying Bitcoin

One of the best things about cryptocurrencies is that you can transfer them anywhere in the world. You can also purchase and trade them if you're not in the U.S. or using U.S. dollars.

This chapter consists of a guide that is a comprehensive, but not exhaustive, list of where you can buy bitcoin anywhere in the world with the local currency.

Nearly everywhere in the world, you can use LocalBitcoins, Bisq, or a bitcoin ATM. But first, it's important to tell you how governments are attempting to wage a new war on bitcoin.

The New "War on Bitcoin"

Early in 2017, the Venezuelan government revoked Surbitcoin's bank account of. Surbitcoin is the country's largest bitcoin exchange.

It forced the company to suspend operations. And bitcoin owners who used the service had nowhere to store their currency.

That same month, the Chinese government issued a string of new policies to crack down on bitcoin exchanges.

Similarly, Chinese bitcoin owners were left without services to buy, sell, or store their cryptocurrencies.

In both cases, repressive governments were trying to prevent money from leaving their countries.

That's because China and Venezuela have strict capital controls. These policies restrict the free flow of cash in and out of their countries.

It's no wonder their people turned to bitcoin to circumvent these heavy-handed policies. But now, these governments are targeting bitcoin. It's no surprise as bitcoin is one of the best defenses against the War on Cash...

The War on Cash is an offensive by governments around the world to control how you use your money and tax every cent you own...

The latest assault is against bitcoin exchanges.

But that doesn't mean people in these countries can no longer buy bitcoin. I'll show you a simple (and legal) way people in China, Venezuela, and other countries can use to trade bitcoins without using exchanges.

Because these crackdowns aren't just happening in socialist countries. We're seeing them sprout up in America, too...

Crackdowns in America

In September 2016, the Hawaii Division of Financial Institutions passed a new regulation that forced Coinbase (America's leading bitcoin exchange) to cease operating in the state.

The policy requires Coinbase to maintain cash reserves equal to the digital currency funds it holds for customers. (So, if a Hawaii resident holds $1,000 worth of bitcoin, Coinbase would have to match those funds with cash.)

That's like asking a brokerage firm to match its clients' funds.

Right now, TD Ameritrade has $1.7 billion in cash and short-term investments. But client assets are $774 billion.

Can you imagine asking TD Ameritrade to put up another $772 billion to match its clients' funds?

That's essentially what Hawaii wants Coinbase to do. In response, Coinbase has suspended operations in Hawaii.

And it's not just Hawaii. As the "War on Bitcoin" heats up, your state could be next...

In this chapter, we'll show you a safe way to hold your bitcoins if Coinbase (or some other exchange) leaves your state.

When One Road Is Blocked, Find Another

Misguided policies like Hawaii's are inevitable as bitcoin gains mainstream legitimacy.

Eventually, governments will have no choice but to accept bitcoin as an alternative currency. As we've said before, it's here to stay.

But in the meantime, we'll show you other places Americans can trade bitcoins.

When their exchanges closed, Chinese and Venezuelan bitcoin owners turned to a service called LocalBitcoins.

Soon after China announced its new bitcoin exchange policies in February, trading volume on LocalBitcoins nearly quadrupled. And in Venezuela, it exploded after the crackdown (see chart on the next page).

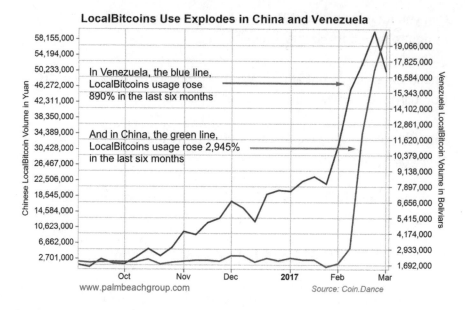

LocalBitcoins Use Explodes in China and Venezuela

In Venezuela, the blue line, LocalBitcoins usage rose 890% in the last six months

And in China, the green line, LocalBitcoins usage rose 2,945% in the last six months

www.palmbeachgroup.com

Source: Coin.Dance

If your country or state places restrictions on bitcoin trading, LocalBitcoins is a service you can turn to.

Here's How It Works

LocalBitcoins is a peer-to-peer bitcoin trading website. You can use it to buy bitcoins online or in person. And you can pay for it with gift cards, MoneyGram, PayPal, or by cash deposit at a bank.

LocalBitcoins is easy to use. In fact, it took me less than an hour to make my first trade...

I chose to deposit cash at a local bank. Now that may sound risky... but LocalBitcoins has an escrow feature to protect buyers and sellers (more on that in a moment).

First, I registered on the website. That allowed me to search for buyers and sellers. Each has a feedback score. (It's similar to the customer ratings you see on Amazon.)

Once I found a seller, I verified his personal information on LocalBitcoins. After we agreed to terms, I could use LocalBitcoins' escrow service to complete the online transactions.

When the transaction is initiated, the seller's bitcoin is placed in escrow. That means the buyer doesn't have to worry about being scammed. If the bitcoin is in escrow, he can purchase them. If not, he can walk away.

But the bitcoin doesn't get released until the seller confirms payment. That means the seller doesn't have to worry about the buyer taking the bitcoin without paying up.

I chose a seller with a 100% feedback rating who used a convenient local bank. The price wasn't the lowest, but it was fair... roughly a 4% premium to the Bitcoin price.

The seller provided deposit instructions. After making the deposit, I provided a copy of the receipt and a picture of my ID. It was all done through the LocalBitcoins website.

By the way, not all transactions require an ID. It depends on the seller and the payment method. Make sure to read the terms of the agreement before making a trade.

The bitcoins were deposited directly into my LocalBitcoins wallet. And I transferred them out with no problem. The entire transaction took less than an hour.

I suggest you spend some time researching the website before using it. The site includes a search function that separates offers by amount, currency, location, and offer type.

Based on my experience, LocalBicoins is easy to use and the price is fair.

As of publishing, LocalBitcoins is available in 248 countries and 14,766 cities.

Bisq

Like LocalBitcoins, Bisq (formerly Bitsquare) is a decentralized bitcoin exchange. At the time of this writing, Bisq supports the following currencies:

- Australian dollar
- Bahraini dinar
- Brazilian real
- British pound
- Cambodian riel
- Canadian dollar
- Chinese yuan
- Costa Rican colón
- Euros
- Israeli new shekel
- Japanese yen
- New Zealand dollar
- Norwegian krone
- Polish zloty
- Swedish krona
- Swiss franc
- U.S. dollar

Bitcoin ATMs

The best way to find a Bitcoin ATM near you is to conduct a Google search. Please be aware of the fees that apply for using a Bitcoin ATM.

Country Availability for Recommended Services

Please note: These services are adding to their list of available countries. Be sure to check their websites for the most updated lists.

The Gemini exchange is available in the following areas:

- Canada
- Hong Kong
- Singapore
- South Korea
- United Kingdom
- United States (all states except Alaska, Arizona, Hawaii, Michigan, Oregon, and Washington)

Coinbase is available in the following countries:

- Australia*
- Austria
- Belgium
- Bulgaria
- Canada*
- Croatia
- Cyprus
- Czech Republic
- Denmark
- Finland
- France
- Greece
- Hungary
- Ireland
- Italy
- Latvia
- Liechtenstein
- Malta
- Monaco
- Netherlands
- Norway
- Poland
- Portugal
- Romania

- San Marino
- Singapore
- Slovakia
- Slovenia
- Spain
- Sweden
- Switzerland
- United States
- United Kingdom

*At the time of publishing, Coinbase only supports buying in Australia and Canada. It's working to support selling as well.

Abra is available in the following countries:

- Philippines
- United States

Abra is working on adding more countries. Check their website periodically for updates.

Other Ways to Buy Bitcoin in Your Country

This section goes country by country and covers services that allow you to buy bitcoin with your local currency.

This is for informational purposes and does not include official recommendations. Before you use any service, take some time to learn about it and see what others are saying about it. Then, if you decide to use a service, test it out with small transactions first.

Canada

- **Direct:** Both Kraken and Coinbase are open for Canadian customers who can buy bitcoins with bank transfers or credit cards and store them on the platform's online wallet. Also, Indacoin is available for Canadian customers. More specifically for Canadians, however, are QuickBT and Canadian Bitcoins, platforms where you can directly buy bitcoin up to 150 Canadian dollars with several means of payment like Interac Online and Flexepin vouchers. Canadian Bitcoins also offers the option to pay with cash in person or by deposit.

- **P2P:** Canadian customers can use international P2P markets like Paxful and LocalBitcoins to buy bitcoins.

- **Exchange:** Several exchanges support trade with Canadian dollars. Kraken, QuadrigaCX, and Coinsquare are the most prominent examples.

Mexico

- **Gift Cards:** With the Chip-Chap app, you can buy bitcoin gift cards at more than 5,000 shops.

-
- **Direct:** Volabit allows people to buy bitcoin with Mexican pesos by bank transfers or cash deposits at OXXO, 7-Eleven, and Banamex branches and ATMs.

-
- **Exchange:** Bitso is an exchange for Mexico. Fees are rapidly decreasing with trade volume to as low as 0.1%; the spread is relatively small.

Central and South America

Several exchanges are available in some South and Central American countries. SatoshiTango is a direct vendor for Brazil, Chile, Colombia, Costa Rica, Ecuador, El Salvador, Guatemala, Honduras, Mexico, Nicaragua, Panama, and Peru. Bitex offers services in Argentina, Chile, Colombia, and Uruguay.

Local P2P bitcoin markets are available in most Latin American countries.

Brazil

- **Direct:** People living in Brazil can buy bitcoins directly at <u>Mercado Bitcoin</u>, a broker calling itself the biggest bitcoin exchange in Latin America.

- **Exchange:** One major bitcoin exchange in Brazil is <u>FlowBTC</u>. Here, users can buy or sell bitcoins. Deposits can be made with bank transfers. Another major exchange is <u>Foxbit</u>.

Argentina

- **Direct:** Ripio is a wallet app that lets users buy bitcoins. Its special feature is that it allows users to purchase bitcoins on credit and serves as a payment gateway to pay with bitcoin.

Venezuela

- **Exchange:** Venezuela has its own bitcoin exchange called <u>SurBitcoin</u>.

Chile

- **Exchange:** Chile has its own bitcoin exchange, SurBTC, which hit international news when it received funding from the Chilean government. People can buy or sell bitcoins here and make deposits in Chilean pesos with local bank transfers. <u>SurBTC</u> is also available in Columbia and Peru.

Europe

- **ATM:** The website <u>Coin ATM Radar</u> lists hundreds of bitcoin ATMs in Europe.

- **Direct:** Due to the unclear state of regulation in the eurozone, there are a dozen direct exchanges to buy bitcoin that offer a variety of payment channels. Most of these brokers charge their customers fees of 0.5–5% depending on the payment channel and earn by the spread. **Examples in alphabetical order:**

  - Anycoin Direct (SEPA, Sofort, Giropay, iDeal, MyBank, TrustPay)
  - Bitit (Neosurf prepaid voucher, not available in every country)
  - BitPanda (SEPA, Sofort, Skrill, credit card, Neteller, PayPal)
  - BTCDirect (SEPA, Sofort, credit card, Giropay, Neteller)
  - Coinify (SEPA, credit card, PayPal)
  - CoinMate (Sofort, SEPA, MoneyPolo)
  - HappyCoins (Sofort, iDeal, Mister Cash, SEPA, Giropay, MyBank)
  - Indacoin (credit card)
  - SpectroCoin (Sofort, Giropay, iDeal, Perfect Money, SEPA)

While the platforms above just sell bitcoin and offer no advanced online wallet—or no wallet at all—the Coinbase online wallet has the option to buy bitcoin via bank transfer or credit card and is available in most European countries.

- **P2P:** LocalBitcoins is available for every country in the eurozone except Germany. Bitcoin.de is a P2P marketplace for the whole eurozone where people can buy and sell bitcoins with SEPA transfers. With 0.5% fees and a low spread, Bitcoin.de is likely the cheapest method to buy bitcoins outside exchanges.

- **Exchange:** Several exchanges serve the eurozone. Kraken is the leading exchange followed by Bitstamp and <u>BTC-E</u>. All exchanges demand full Know Your Client (KYC) forms to ensure you have all the details.

Austria

Citizens of Austria can buy bitcoins with gift cards from <u>Bitcoinbon</u> that are sold in many traffic shops. This is an easy but relatively expensive way to buy bitcoins.

Germany

For Germans, the <u>Fidor Bank</u> is a good place to start buying bitcoins. This online bank partners with Bitcoin.de and Kraken, making trading on these platforms significantly faster and easier. On Bitcoin.de, Fidor customers can immediately achieve full KYC status and use the so-called ExpressTrade. This allows them to buy an unlimited amount of bitcoins for relatively low prices only minutes after the first contact with the platform.

Spain

In Spain, you can easily buy bitcoins at thousands of ATMs with <u>Bit2Me</u> and <u>Chip-Chap</u>.

United Kingdom

- **Direct:** Coinbase is available for U.K. citizens to buy bitcoins with bank transfers and credit cards. Many people from the U.K. use <u>Bittylicious</u>, which offers bank transfers and credit cards, in addition to U.K.-specific payment options like Paym or Barclays Pingit. However, depending on the payment option, the fees can be quite large.

- **Exchange:** The most popular exchange in the U.K. is <u>Coinfloor</u> followed by <u>Kraken</u> and Coinbase's <u>GDAX</u>.

Switzerland

- **ATM:** Recently, the Swedish national railway company SBB announced that citizens could buy bitcoins at any ticket machine in every rail station. Payment can be made with cash or electronic cash; credit cards are not accepted. On top of this, people in Switzerland can find bitcoin ATMs operated by <u>Bitcoin Suisse</u> in several places.

- **Direct:** The broker Bitcoin Suisse offers the option to buy bitcoins with cash and bank transfer. <u>247exchange</u> offers options to buy bitcoin as well.

Poland

- **Exchanges:** Poland has three bitcoin exchanges where you can buy bitcoins: <u>BitMarket</u>, <u>BitBay</u>, and <u>Bitmaszyna</u>. pl. They offer relatively good conditions to buy bitcoins with zloty.

Norway

- **Direct:** In Norway, you can buy bitcoin with krones using <u>Cubits</u>.

- **Exchange:** Norway has one exchange, <u>Bitcoins Norway</u>. But the volume is quite low, resulting in higher premiums.

Sweden

- **Direct:** Sweden has two Bitcoin brokers you can use to buy bitcoin with kronas: <u>BTCX</u> and <u>FYB-SE</u>.

Denmark

- **Direct:** The only Danish exchange is <u>Coinify</u>.

Ukraine

- **ATM:** With <u>Btcu.biz</u>, users can buy bitcoins at many bank ATMs in Ukraine.

- **Direct:** <u>The Kuna Exchange</u> offers a direct exchange of bitcoin for hryvnas. Another direct exchange is <u>Btcu.biz</u>.

- **Exchange:** With the <u>Kuna Exchange</u>, Ukraine has its own bitcoin exchange for hryvnas.

Russia

- **Direct:** <u>Matbea</u> is a direct vendor of bitcoin for rubles. It requires users to register with their phone numbers.

- **Exchange:** <u>BTC-E</u> is the major exchange to trade rubles and bitcoin. It works with a variety of payment providers to allow the deposit of funds. Another popular exchange in Russia is MaRSe.

Asia

Asia is the fastest-growing market for bitcoin. In China, Japan, and South Korea, there's a vibrant bitcoin trade on exchanges. But countries like the United Arab Emirates are more or less bitcoin-free. In these countries, your best chance is to find an ATM or sellers on <u>LocalBitcoins</u>.

China

- **Exchanges:** China has some of the most liquid bitcoin exchanges in the world. <u>Huobi</u>, <u>OKCoin</u>, and <u>BTC China</u> have the biggest volume.

Japan

- **Direct:** The most popular direct exchange broker for yen is bitFlyer. The broker offers a wide range of verification degrees—including emailing your full KYC form—and charges very low fees.

- **Exchange:** Quoine, Coincheck, and Kraken are three exchanges that serve the Japanese market.

Thailand

- **Direct:** One bitcoin broker for Thailand is bitcoin.co.th. Another is coins.co.th, and it also includes an easy-to-use online wallet.

- **Exchange:** Thailand has its own bitcoin exchange, bx.in.th.

South Korea

- **Direct and ATM:** Coinplug offers a variety of services to buy and sell bitcoins. It provides two unique ATMs in Seoul and enable the purchase of bitcoin in thousands of ATMs in the country by partnering with an ATM producer. They also provide the option to buy bitcoins with several gift cards.

- **Exchange:** With Korbit, South Korea has a well-developed exchange that offers not only trading with bitcoin, but also wallets for all devices and a remittance service. Coinplug has an exchange as well.

India

- **Direct:** India's biggest bitcoin vendor where you can buy, sell, save, and send bitcoin is Unocoin. There's also

Zebpay, another big platform for bitcoins in India. Like every exchange in India, those two platforms require an identity verification.

- **Exchange:** Coinsecure is both an online wallet and an exchange.

Philippines

- **Gift Cards:** On Prepaid Bitcoin, you can redeem voucher cards you buy in several locations in the Philippines.

- **Direct:** BuyBitcoin and Coins.ph are two bitcoin vendors. Coins.ph accepts a wide spectrum of payment channels like cash deposits at banks, online transfers, and vouchers available in stores nationwide.

- **Exchanges:** The Philippines has two Bitcoin exchanges: Coinage and BTCExchange.

Turkey

- **Gift Cards:** With Bitupcard, you can buy a voucher and redeem it for bitcoins online.

- **Direct:** Koinim is a platform where you can directly buy bitcoin and Litecoin with lira. .

- **Exchange:** BTC Turk is Turkey's first Bitcoin exchange. Here, you can buy and sell bitcoins.

Malaysia

- **Direct:** In Malaysia CoinBox and coins.my provide an online wallet and an easy method to buy and sell bitcoins.

- **Exchange:** <u>Coinhako</u> is a wallet with the option to buy and sell for Malaysia and **Singapore**. <u>Luno</u> offers an exchange for Malaysia and Indonesia.

Vietnam

- **Direct:** In Vietnam, you can buy bitcoin at <u>Bitcoin Vietnam</u>.

- **Exchange:** <u>VBTC</u> is Vietnam's major bitcoin exchange.

Indonesia

- **Direct:** You can also buy bitcoins at <u>Bitcoin.co.id</u>.

- **Exchange:** <u>Luno</u> offers an exchange for Indonesia and Malaysia.

Taiwan

- **Direct:** Citizens of Taiwan can use <u>MaiCoin</u> to buy, sell, and use bitcoins.

Israel

- **Direct:** <u>Bits of Gold</u> is the oldest bitcoin platform in Israel. Here, you can directly buy and sell bitcoins.

- **Exchange:** <u>Bit2C</u> is Israel's major bitcoin exchange.

United Arab Emirates

- **Direct:** Citizens of the United Arab Emirates can use <u>BitOasis</u> to buy bitcoins directly.

Kuwait

- **Direct:** In Kuwait, you can buy bitcoins on BitFils.

Australia

- **Direct:** Australia has several direct bitcoin vendors: Bit Trade Australia supports POLi Payments; buyabitcoin.com.au accepts cash deposits from banks; CoinTree supports both POLi Payments and cash deposits from banks; CoinLoft supports POLi Payments, cash deposits from banks, and Flexepin vouchers; bitcoin.com.au allows users to acquire bitcoin by depositing cash at kiosks; CoinJar offers ways to buy bitcoin and an easy-to-use wallet.

- **Exchange:** Independent Reserve and CoinSpot are the two major bitcoin exchanges in Australia.

New Zealand

- **Direct:** With both Coined and buybitcoin.co.nz, you can buy bitcoins through your bank; Coinhub allows you to not only pay with bank transfers, but also with cash deposits at ATMs and through PayPal; MyBitcoinSaver offers a wallet and the option to invest regularly in bitcoins with automatic bank transfers.

- **Exchange:** New Zealand has one bitcoin exchange: NZBCX.

South Africa

- **Exchange:** South Africa has two bitcoin exchanges: Luno and Ice3x.

Nigeria

- **Direct:** In Nigeria, you can use <u>NairaEx</u> to buy bitcoins with bank transfers or <u>BitPesa</u> to purchase coins with debit cards or Paga.

- **Exchange:** In Nigeria, you can use the <u>Luno</u> exchange.

Tanzania

- **Direct:** In Tanzania, you can use <u>BitPesa</u> to buy bitcoins with bank transfers.

Uganda

- **Direct:** In Uganda, <u>BitPesa</u> allows citizen to buy bitcoins with MTN Uganda or Airtel Money.

Chapter 15:
The Comprehensive Crypto FAQ

Still not sure about this cryptocurrency thing? Let us part ways with a comprehensive FAQ to fill in any gaps this book may have left...

Crypto Basics

What is a cryptocurrency?

A cryptocurrency is a digital currency that uses cryptography for security. This feature also makes cryptocurrencies virtually anonymous to use.

In essence, a cryptocurrency is a piece of computer code that can be used as a medium of exchange, or in some cases as a store of value. In other words, you can use them to buy things or hold them as investments.

Because they are digital, cryptocurrencies make transactions faster and more efficient. For instance, you can use them to transfer funds to other people.

Unlike fiat currencies (dollars, yen, euros, etc.), cryptocurrencies are not issued by governments or central banks. That makes them immune to government manipulation.

Most cryptocurrencies can only be bought with bitcoin, although a few larger ones can be bought with fiat currencies.

How many cryptocurrencies are there?

At the time of writing, according to the website coinmarketcap.com, there are 946 cryptocurrencies.

What is an App Coin?

A cryptocurrency is the digital equivalent of cash. It's used to buy things.

Application coins (App Coins), or tokens, are native to decentralized applications. They can be used to run the application. They may also represent digital assets. And, in other cases, they are the digital equivalent of a stock.

There are coins in development that will be backed by hard assets such as gold and silver.

And then there are tokens that represent digital shares in the company.

What is a Blockchain?

A blockchain is the underlying technology for cryptocurrencies. Put simply, a blockchain is an online digital ledger. It's used to track and record cryptocurrency transactions.

Because it is efficient, secure, and hard to hack, blockchain technology is expanding to other industries. Soon, you will be able to record and track any type of transaction—from car titles to insurance contracts—on the blockchain.

That's one of the reasons we're so bullish on this technology.

What backs cryptocurrencies?

That's a question to ask on a case-by-case basis. Real assets may back some cryptos. Others might represent claims against future profits. It all depends on the cryptocurrency or App Coin.

For bitcoin, there is no intrinsic value. It's not backed by any government. Its value is derived by its use.

It continues to be used more and more. The chart below shows the growth in daily bitcoin transactions. We've gone from 50,000 transactions per day to 300,000 per day in five years.

Bitcoin Daily Transaction Volume

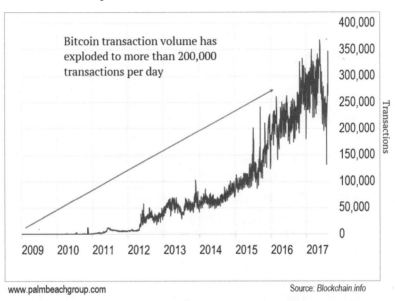

www.palmbeachgroup.com   Source: *Blockchain.info*

Many people have a hard time getting past the fact it's not backed by a government. There's no rule that a currency needs to be backed by a government, but it's all we've ever known.

Remember, money is nothing more than a social contract: a representation of value between two parties. Bitcoin can serve that function just as easily as any government-backed currency.

Friedrich Hayek predicted in 1976 that private currencies would one day take over government issued currencies. He was right, and it has started.

How do I buy, sell, and store cryptocurrencies and App Coins?

You can buy and sell cryptocurrencies and App Coins on a cryptocurrency exchange, and store them in a cryptocurrency wallet.

We've recommended exchanges and wallets. In some cases, an exchange may not available where you live. So, we have several to choose from.

Read the earlier chapters of this book to learn more about them.

What is the difference between a cryptocurrency exchange and a cryptocurrency wallet?

An exchange is where you can buy and sell cryptocurrencies. A wallet is where you store your cryptocurrencies.

For security reasons, we recommend you hold most of your cryptocurrencies in a wallet rather than an exchange. You should only keep the amount of money you plan to use to purchase other cryptocurrencies on an exchange.

That's because the exchanges can be targets for hackers.

All the exchanges we use take proper measures to ensure the safety of your funds. Nevertheless, it's safer to hold your funds in a wallet where you control the private keys.

Again, refer to previous chapters to learn more about wallets and exchanges.

Why do you recommend so many cryptocurrency services?

When it comes to financial services, we're used to an all-in-one experience. Today, you can easily fulfill all your financial service needs with just one company like a bank or brokerage firm.

But it's not like that with cryptocurrencies. The industry is only about 10 years old. And it's rapidly developing. In the future, we expect it will be much easier to buy and sell cryptocurrencies. Eventually, there'll be a one-stop shop for them.

Until then, the best thing we can do is be flexible. And that means not relying on just one service.

Investing in Cryptocurrency

Do you have to buy bitcoin to buy every other cryptocurrency?

In nearly all cases, you will need to buy bitcoin to purchase other cryptocurrencies.

Bitcoin is the reserve currency of cryptocurrencies. All cryptocurrencies are priced in bitcoin and can be bought with bitcoin.

There are now some opportunities to purchase other cryptocurrencies using ether. At the time of this writing, Kraken has that option for some of the other cryptocurrencies on its exchange.

Is there an easy way to find out the most up-to-date conversion rate for bitcoin to U.S. dollars?

Yes. You can use this handy calculator from CoinDesk at coindesk.com/calculator. Type in the amount of bitcoin, small or large, and it will automatically calculate how much the bitcoin is worth in U.S. dollars. Or vice versa, if you type the amount in the U.S. dollar box.

How can I track daily cryptocurrency prices?

CoinMarketCap is the best website for tracking daily prices.

How can I purchase cryptocurrencies without a smartphone?

For those without a smartphone, we recommend that you use the Gemini Exchange or Coinbase. Alternatively, you can also try LocalBitcoins or a Bitcoin ATM. Read the previous chapters for more information.

Can I buy bitcoin in currencies other than the U.S. dollar?

LocalBitcoins allows you to buy bitcoin anyplace in the world. The Kraken exchange allows deposits in euros, yen, and Canadian dollars. And Coinbase is now available in 33 countries. See our list of exchanges here for all options.

This website is also a good source for buying bitcoin around the world: https://blockgeeks.com/guides/how-to-buy-bitcoin/

Can I buy cryptocurrencies or App Coins through my broker?

No. You can only buy cryptocurrencies and App Coins on a cryptocurrency exchange.

If you try to buy a cryptocurrency through a traditional broker, you'll end up owning something completely different. For example, the symbol for ether is ETH. If you buy that from a broker, you'll end up with shares of the furniture company Ethan Allen.

Is there a minimum investment to get started?

No. You can buy $1 worth of bitcoin if you want. Each bitcoin is divisible to the eighth decimal.

How much should I invest in cryptocurrencies?

We recommend allocating no more than 5% of your total net investable assets in cryptocurrencies. From there, you can take even smaller positions in each individual cryptocurrency recommendation.

Remember: It doesn't take much to turn a small stake of $100, $500, or even $1,000 into life-changing wealth.

To spread the risk, do you recommend someone buy four or five cryptocurrencies?

We recommend you own a uniform dollar amount of all the coins that are still actionable in the model portfolio. We suggest capping position sizes at $200–$400 per position for smaller investors and $500–$1,000 per position for larger investors.

I have several different cryptocurrency exchanges and apps. How do I manage them all?

We understand it can be a hassle overseeing several portfolios. The best advice we can give is to be organized.

For example, you can create a new folder on your browser and bookmark the cryptocurrency websites you use. Then start a file on the cryptocurrency services. Use it to keep information such as usernames and passwords. To keep tabs on your portfolio, you can create an Excel spreadsheet.

We track our portfolios through an app called <u>Blockfolio</u>. It's easy to use and a quick way to know your portfolio value at a moment's notice.

Can all cryptocurrencies be held in the same digital wallet, or do you need different ones for different currencies?

As of today, there is no one wallet that can hold all cryptocurrencies. But we imagine in the future there will be. One company working on this is Jaxx. In addition to BTC, the Jaxx wallet holds ETH, DASH, ETC, REP, LTC, and ZEC.

- For BTC, we use Abra, Airbitz, Blockchain.info, Coinbase, and Jaxx

- For ETH, you can use Coinbase, Jaxx, or MyEtherWallet.

- For XMR, you can use the MyMonero wallet.

- SteemPower can be stored on the Steemit platform.

What is the typical hold period for a cryptocurrency?

It's difficult to give precise timing. We've sold portions of our holdings in the past. Right now, even though we're sitting on some nice gains, we still see upside ahead.

When the time is right, we'll take profits. But we'll also keep a portion of our holdings for the long term.

Think about early Microsoft investors. They could have sold for a profit of 100%, 500%, even 1,000%. Hopefully they held a little because Microsoft went on to return over 60,000%.

Can you spend cryptocurrencies?

Yes. More than 100,000 merchants accept bitcoin. Some merchants accept bitcoin directly from your wallet.

If you need to convert your bitcoins into dollars before spending them, you can open a bitcoin debit card on Xapo.

And you can use the Purse app to make bitcoin purchases on Amazon.

How do you exchange cryptocurrency for spendable cash or can you only spend money in the crypto system?

There are plenty of ways to go in and out of the system at will.

There are many merchants that accept bitcoin. Look or search for the "bitcoin accepted here" sign. You can send bitcoin from any wallet, even an exchange wallet. But it's best to use your personal wallet.

Then there's sites like Purse.io. At Purse, you can purchase and bid on Amazon goods with bitcoin.

If you need to pay in dollars, then check out Xapo (https://xapo.com/card/). Xapo is a debit card you fund with bitcoin and spend in dollars. It works anywhere Visa is accepted, and you can even connect your Xapo debit card to PayPal.

Why did bitcoin never become a stock?

Bitcoin is a currency, not a stock. If you want to invest in a blockchain company, you would buy its App Coin.

Can one buy cryptocurrencies with a 401(k) or traditional or Roth IRA?

Yes, you can buy cryptocurrencies in a self-directed 401(k) or IRA. BitcoinIRA is a company that specializes in bitcoin IRAs and can answer questions about the process.

Are there any cryptocurrency exchange-traded Funds (ETFs)?

At the time of this writing, there are none. But some are in the works.

Navigating the Exchanges

What if I can't find my bank listed in one of the services you recommend for buying bitcoin with local currency?

Your options depend on the service you use. Below, we go through each service.

For the Gemini Exchange:

Go to Bank Settings. On that page, you'll see a section to add a new bank. On the pull-down menu, the last option is, "Do not see your bank on the list?" Click on that option and hit continue.

Gemini provides the following instructions so you can get your bank listed.

Instant Bank Verification Not Supported, Wire Verification Required

Unfortunately, your bank is not supported by our instant verification system. In order to verify your bank account and link it to your Gemini account, you will need to first complete a wire transfer into your Gemini account. Once your identity information is verified, you may transfer USD in and out of your Gemini account by navigating to Transfer Funds. We will credit your Gemini account $20 to offset the wire fee you may incur from your initial wire.

After your first successful wire deposit, you will have the ability to set up bank transfers (via ACH).

After completing a wire transfer, your bank will then be verified for ACH transfers.

For Coinbase:

On Coinbase, you can add a bank if it's not listed as well. Go to Settings, then click on Payment Methods. Then, find and click the "Add Payment Method" button. Next, click "Bank Account." Coinbase will display a list of banks. Choose "Other Bank."

Coinbase will prompt you to fill in information including your name, routing number, and account number. See the picture below for reference.

For Abra:

With the Abra app, you can only use the listed banks.

You can check for an up-to-date list of supported banks at: abra.
zendesk.com.

For Airbitz:

Airbitz uses a service called Glidera for converting local currency
into bitcoin. Like Abra, your bank needs to be listed.

You can find an up-to-date list of supported banks at: www.glidera.
io/supportbanks.

How do I transfer from bitcoin to other coins using Gemini?

You would transfer your bitcoin from Gemini to an exchange like
Bittrex.

Before you initiate a transfer on Gemini, you'll need your wallet
address at Bittrex.

- At Bittrex, click on the "Wallets" tab at the top right of
  the webpage. In the search bar, type in BTC for bitcoin.
  That will pull up your bitcoin wallet. You'll see a plus sign
  and a minus sign next to your bitcoin wallet. Click on the
  plus sign to get your bitcoin address. Copy your address
  and go back to Gemini.

At Gemini, start by clicking on the "Transfer Funds" tab. Then select
"Withdraw from exchange" from the pull-down window and then
"BTC" from the next pull-down menu. Paste your address from
Bittrex into the "Destination Address" field. Then fill in the amount
of bitcoin you want to send. Then click "Review Withdrawal." You'll
get a chance to review the details before finalized the transaction.

Transfers generally take 10 minutes but could take longer if the network is congested.

One day you are recommending Abra over Coinbase, and the next day it's Gemini. Are there reasons for choosing one over the other?

When it comes to financial services, we're used to the all-in-one experience. Today you can easily fulfill all your financial service needs with just one company.

But it's not like that in the cryptocurrency space. Remember, the whole industry isn't even a decade old. But it's rapidly developing, and it's not hard to imagine that it will be much easier in the future.

Until then, the best thing we can do is be flexible. And that means not relying on just one service.

For those just starting, figuring out the cryptocurrency ecosystem can be daunting. So, I'll give a brief recap here to alleviate some of the confusion. Keep in mind—and this is very important—most services serve more than one function. As an example, Coinbase is both a wallet and a way to convert USD to bitcoin.

The Exchanges

- Gemini – Can deposit USD; BTC and ETH are the only cryptos you can buy

- Bittrex – No USD deposit; offers over 130 cryptos to buy (all in BTC)

- Kraken - Can deposit USD; In addition to BTC and ETH, offers 13 cryptos you can buy. Some can be purchased with ETH.

The Wallets

- Abra – App only; deposit USD; holds BTC only

- Airbitz – App only; deposit USD; holds BTC only

- Blockchain.info – PC and smartphone app; cannot deposit USD (but reportedly coming soon); holds BTC only

- Coinbase – PC and smartphone app; can deposit USD; holds BTC and ETH

- Jaxx – PC and smartphone app; cannot deposit USD; holds BTC, ETH, DASH, ETC, REP, LTC, and ZEC

Exchange Fees

- At Bittrex, the trading fees are 0.25%.

- At Kraken, fees depend on volume and whether you're the maker or taker. The highest charge is 0.26%.

- At Gemini, fees depend on volume and whether you're the maker or taker. The highest charge is 0.25%. 0.25% translates to 50 cents on a $200 purchase.

Conversion Fees

- Gemini – free to transfer

- Abra – free to transfer

- Airbitz – 1.1%

- Coinbase – 1.5%

Will there ever be a "one size fits all" crypto trading exchange?

Yes, but it's a few years away.

Is it possible to move currencies from one exchange to another?

Yes. Let's say you're transferring bitcoin from Gemini to Bittrex. Go to Bittrex and copy your deposit address. Then, go to Gemini where you'll do a withdrawal to your Bittrex account.

Risks and Good Practices

What are the risks involved with buying and holding cryptocurrencies?

The biggest risks to holding cryptocurrencies are actually user-inflicted.

The most common mistakes are losing private keys or passwords or making errors in transferring, buying, or selling cryptocurrencies.

New users should test out services with small amounts first before they feel comfortable buying cryptocurrencies.

There are other risks: Exchanges can be hacked and all the currency on the site can be stolen. Or a wallet provider could go out of business and the currency it holds could be lost.

How are cryptocurrencies different from pump-and-dump Ponzi schemes?

Like any other investment (real estate, stocks, antiques, etc.), there will be fraud. That's true for cryptocurrencies as well.

That's why we put so many man-hours of research into our

cryptocurrencies. There are more than 900 cryptocurrencies out there. We do all the hard work to separate the great ones from the frauds.

In the early days of bitcoin, several exchanges went bankrupt and stuck the investors with huge losses. What is the probability of that happening today with other cryptos?

Not quite several, just one: Mt. Gox in 2014. Bitfinex was also hacked in 2016, but those investors were eventually made whole.

We haven't seen any major exchange hacks since then. So, that shows the exchange providers are taking security seriously and have learned from past mistakes.

What advantages do cryptocurrencies have over physical gold?

Cryptocurrencies can be moved anywhere in an instant and there's no storage costs.

If the world returned to a gold standard, would bitcoin still be valuable?

Yes, people would still use bitcoin. If we returned to a gold standard, it would have to be government mandated.

The idea of not having a record "on paper" or having something I can hold (like gold) bothers me. How do you reassure old-timers and technophobes like me?

If you're an old timer, you've learned one thing by now. Life always changes. We'll show you everything you need to know. And just invest what you're comfortable with.

What's to stop someone from creating unlimited cryptocurrencies?

Nothing. Unlimited cryptocurrencies can be invented just like unlimited fiat currencies can be invented. The cryptocurrencies that aren't used much will have little value.

What will prevent an endless cycle of new cryptos coming into the marketplace, degrading/destroying the value of their predecessors?

It's a mistake to think a new crypto degrades the value of other cryptos. It's like saying since a new business opened, all businesses in existence are now worth less.

There's going to be thousands, if not millions, of cryptos. Some will be backed by real assets. Some will not have any inherent backing and will be valued based on their use. Cryptos are something that could have very micro uses, thus so many.

How does one avoid money being stolen on a scam crypto that has no real market or use?

The easiest way is to follow our advice at Palm Beach Research Group.

Can cryptocurrencies be spoofed and what is the protection against hackers?

I haven't seen a crypto be spoofed but anything is possible. Your best protection against hackers is to use strong passwords along with two-factor authentication.

Can banks flag your account if you transfer money to Gemini?

We've had no reports from subscribers of this happening.

To what extent does the government have access to our bitcoin purchase records?

With the appropriate resources, I imagine they can find out anything they want.

How come we need a "wallet" on top of a trading platform?

For security purposes, you'll want to hold most your cryptocurrencies in a wallet rather than an exchange.

Any exchange is a natural target for hackers, as the exchange brings in funds from millions of individuals.

All the exchanges we use take proper security measures to ensure the safety of your funds. Nevertheless, it's more prudent to hold your funds in a wallet where you control the private keys.

What happens if the internet goes down due to terrorism or political upheaval?

If the internet goes down, cryptocurrencies should be the least of your concerns. The entire modern world, banks, hospitals, and governments rely on the internet. No one entity can take down the whole internet.

If the overall market crashes, what would be the impact on cryptocurrencies?

You'll see more investors flock to bitcoin, and that would bolster the entire crypto market.

Trading Crypto

What factors cause cryptocurrency prices to move up and down?

Just like stocks, cryptocurrencies and App Coins are moved by fundamentals and investor sentiment.

Why does the value of BTC vary from exchange to exchange?

It's a small, inefficient market. We saw the same thing occur in the gold market in the 1960s and 1970s. As more money comes into the market, these differences will start to narrow.

Can cryptocurrencies be "shorted"?

They can, but we don't recommend it.

How do I keep track of the various crypto prices?

Coinmarketcap.com is the best resource for tracking prices.

Where can I find charts on various cryptos on various time scales?

Coinmarketcap.com is also the best resource for charts. Click on the crypto you want to check and the chart pulls up. You can track USD price, BTC price, and market cap. And you can set any time frame you want.

How do I track my performance with cryptos?

Bittrex has a trade history section that you can use to evaluate performance. You can also download your trades to an Excel spreadsheet.

What is the typical trading volume in cryptocurrencies?

Bitcoin's trading volume currently ranges from $10,000 or less per day to over $500 million. Check out coinmarketcap.com to see the daily trading volume for all cryptocurrencies.

Is it easy to enjoy significant returns when the volume is low?

When volume is low, then the price can be more easily moved around by a big trader. That move could be up or down.

How do I determine the best buy and sell signals?

We'll keep you up to date via our monthly issues, updates, and alerts at *Palm Beach Letter*.

What triggers the constant change in value?

The entire cryptocurrency market is around $80 billion at the time of publishing. The value of all the stock exchanges in the world is $70 trillion. So, the cryptocurrency market, overall, is still very small. With less volume and less liquidity, prices are more volatile.

Our observation of cryptocurrency markets is that they're "compressed" compared to stock markets. In other words, patterns that play out over months and weeks in the stock market play out in days and hours in the cryptocurrency market.

How do you hedge against crypto volatility?

Volatility is part of the game and to be expected. We will not be employing any hedging strategies.

Should I sell half of my position on a double and hold the remainder long term?

We will be selling at points and taking profits off the table. But we'll also likely keep a portion of positions for shots at long-term home runs.

Think about an early Microsoft investor. They could have sold for a profit of 100%, 500%, even 1,000%. Hopefully they held a little, because it went on to return over 60,000%.

How much money do you feel would be a good allocation for each cryptocurrency?

We suggest capping position sizes at $200–400 per position for smaller investors and $500–$1,000 per position for larger investors.

Can you leverage cryptocurrencies with options like the dollar?

Yes, there are bitcoin options and futures services, but we don't recommend using leverage.

If a person doesn't have thousands to invest, are cryptos still worth getting into?

Yes. Cryptocurrencies are the future. At least get your foot in the door and buy some bitcoin. Download the Abra app, connect your bank account, buy $20 worth on occasion.

How will cryptos do when the dollar index falls and why?

When the dollar falls, cryptos will be used as a store of value. Bitcoin will be the first crypto they turn to.

Where do you see the sentiment levels with crypto?

The overall sentiment for the cryptocurrency market is very positive. That being said, very few people know about cryptocurrencies.

It's also worth noting sentiment can vary from coin to coin.

Are there technical indicators for crypto?

Sure, the RSI is a technical indicator that you want watch on your cryptos.

Cryptocompare.com is a site where you can find charts with the RSI.

When we buy, we like to see the RSI is over 50, indicating the bulls are in control.

Tax Implications

What are the tax ramifications of investing in cryptocurrencies and profiting from this activity?

Per the IRS, the general rules for property transactions also apply to virtual currencies. You can go to their website for more details.

Are cryptocurrency gains/losses required on your annual tax return?

You should consult your accountant about this.

What is the risk of a government shutting down cryptocurrencies?

Governments can't shut down cryptocurrencies. They can clamp down on the services that make them possible. But even then, users will move to peer-to-peer markets.

And if you hold your coins on your own wallet, no one can take them from you.

Is putting cash in a cryptocurrency equivalent to putting cash in an offshore account as protection from frivolous lawsuits or income tax disputes?

This is a question for your attorney.

Are there any legal restrictions on trading or owning any cryptocurrency? Can you do it as a company? Can you do it in a pension plan?

Institutional accounts are offered at the Gemini Exchange.

There's no reason a pension plan couldn't buy bitcoin or other cryptocurrencies as an investment, as long as it was allowed for in its bylaws.

Are there any tax implications for moving between cryptocurrencies?

Yes, this creates a taxable event.

Looking to the Future

Will bitcoin replace any currency?

I can envision private currencies replacing most fiat currencies. No fiat currency has stood the test of time, anyways.

When will digital currency and banking become the new "normal" and not the exception to the way the U.S. economy functions? Will our system ever be independent of liquid cash?

It's reasonable to think it could happen over a generation. And cash could go as well.

How do you know when a new crypto comes to the market?

When a cryptocurrency comes to market, it's called an initial coin offering, or ICO.

There are various sites that track ICOs:

- https://www.icocountdown.com/
- https://www.ico-list.com/
- https://www.smithandcrown.com/icos/
- https://icotracker.net/
- https://tokenmarket.net/ico-calendar
- https://cryptonomos.com/

Will Forex every play a role in developing future cryptos?

I think it will, but not for a few years yet.

How will cryptos affect the price of gold and silver?

I think the bitcoin vs. gold price will be an interesting narrative for a while. They'll both benefit from reckless central bank policies.

Will bitcoin last?

For anything to have value, it must be relatively scarce and it must be useful.

Bitcoin is both scarce and useful. It is far more useful than any form of currency that has come before.

Bitcoin is the polar opposite of the existing financial system. That makes it a disruptive technology. We know how that story ends...

Chapter 16:
Welcome to the New Renaissance

What lies before us is an economic boom beyond anything we have ever experienced.

Blockchain technology is going to drive efficiency in every aspect of our civilization. It is going to eliminate bureaucracy, middlemen, and cronyism. This will put trillions of dollars back into the economy for productive use.

And the blockchain is going to liberate trillions of dollars in "dead capital"... except it won't be denominated in dollars. It will be denominated in cryptocurrency. These trillions of dollars will be in the hands of real people to do with what they will.

Some of this "extra" money will be fretted away on fleeting consumption. And that's fine. People should be free to spend their own money as they please.

But much of this "extra" money will be used as capital to make our civilization wealthier and more advanced than it has ever been before.

We will see an explosion in energy-related investments that will transform the way we produce and distribute electric power. Energy will become cheaper and more abundant than it has ever been. And the blockchain will make its distribution more efficient than ever before.

Some of this will be from "green" technology such as solar power. But much of it will stem from massive efficiencies in how oil and gas is produced, refined, and distributed.

You will see decentralized power grids on the blockchain. The gains in efficiency and resiliency will be enormous.

Cheap and abundant energy makes everything else cheaper as well. This makes it easy to produce and distribute all the goods and services we use every single day. Which makes our civilization wealthier.

With the blockchain driving efficiency, maximization will no longer be necessary. Right now, people and businesses struggle to squeeze out every dollar of profit because much of their productivity is leeched away by inefficient systems, bureaucracies, and waste.

We will also see a wave of new industries develop. And we will see industries become "self-regulating."

With blockchain-based reputation systems, each industry will have an incentive to produce quality products and provide quality customer service. Just like with individuals, bad businesses will be labeled as such on the blockchain. They won't survive.

You are going to see the regimented, industrial model we all grew up with gradually fade away.

And "jobs" as we know them will be a thing of the past. Now there will still be work and employment... but it will take on a different form.

You see, jobs became an industrial panacea in the 20th century.

The job gave everyone a regimented schedule and a sense of purpose. The job provided a paycheck, a retirement plan, health insurance, life insurance, dental insurance, and numerous other perks in some cases.

Your job made you eligible for your national social insurance program and the gamut of other welfare programs. If you lost your job, then government unemployment benefits would take care of you. If you got hurt and couldn't work, then government disability benefits would take care of you. When you finally retired then government retirement programs would take care of you.

These programs were all tied to your job. The job was made to be central to everyone's life.

All of these things will continue to exist in some capacity... but they will not be tied to the job.

Employment will become much more fluid. Labor and resources will be allocated efficiently to the areas of highest priority, as determined in the marketplace.

That's not true today because we have a whole host of bureaucratic institutions in place, each seeking to direct resources to itself. This creates trillions of dollars' worth of waste and inefficiency. And as we discussed, the blockchain is about to unleash those trillions of dollars.

None of this is utopian. There will still be plenty of problems. And there will inevitably be new problems that pop up as well.

But our increased prosperity, thanks to the blockchain, will make these problems minor compared to the overall benefits.

None of this is hypothetical, either. Everything we need for this economic boom of historic proportions is already here... waiting to be unleashed.

What most people haven't noticed is that technology has been gradually reducing scarcity for one hundred years now. Blockchain technology is going to kick that into hyper-drive.

It required 40% of the U.S. population to work in agriculture to produce enough food to meet demand in the year 1900. Today that number is around 2%, and food is more available than ever before. You can find milk, eggs, meat, fresh fruits, vegetables, and all kinds of other food items at your local grocery store year-round.

Thanks to technological development, oil and gas are now more abundant and cheaper than ever. This has reduced the costs of production and distribution significantly, and it has created competition for the oil cartels and monopolies that have had a strangle-hold on the industry for decades.

Because of this drastic reduction in scarcity, the average person today is far wealthier in standard of living terms than the wealthiest people alive one hundred years ago.

Take a few minutes to walk around your house and catalogue your furniture, appliances, electronics, gadgets, widgets, and stuff.

Most of what you take for granted every single day was not available to your forefathers a short one hundred years ago.

Think about the smartphone, for example.

We tend to take this for granted, but the smartphone in our pocket is far more powerful than the original supercomputers that encompassed entire rooms.

Simply by tapping the touch-screen, we can access the accumulated store of human knowledge instantaneously from nearly anywhere in the developed world. These devices would look like magic wands to our ancestors a few generations back...

Now I don't mean to suggest that we will eliminate scarcity entirely. The constraints of the physical world require energy and labor to produce the goods we consume daily.

But much of the scarcity that currently exists is artificial in nature. It is manufactured by unnecessary restrictions, regulations, bureaucracy, and cronyism.

Blockchain technology will eliminate this waste, and destroy the artificial scarcity. And a new *Renaissance* will follow.

Welcome to the Blockchain Age!